# OLDER

# older

JAMES ROOSE-EVANS

**A Thought Diary**

ZULEIKA

First published 2019
by Zuleika Books & Publishing
Thomas House, 84 Eccleston Square
London, SW1V 1PX

British Library Cataloguing in Publication Data

A catalogue record for this book is
available from the British Library

ISBN: 978-1-99931-258-9

Designed by Euan Monaghan
Printed in England

FOR TONY MORRIS

With deep gratitude for the years of support, encouragement and friendship, and in memory of Hywel Jones, my partner of 54 years.

The theatre director Peter Brook once asked an Indian actor his secret and he replied, 'I try to bring together all that I have experienced in my life, so as to make what I am doing a witness for what I have felt and what I have understood.' As a poet once wrote;

'For you I have come out of myself
To perform life without a mask...
At the deepest level of myself'.

'Life is no brief candle for me. It is a sort of splendid torch and I want to make it burn as brightly as possible before handing it on to future generations.'
*George Bernard Shaw*

'We are never given for ourselves. It is always for others.'
*Llewellyn Vaughan-Williams*

'Planted in the house of the Lord, they will flourish in the courts of our God,
Still bearing fruit when they are old,
Still full of sap, still green, to proclaim that the Lord is just.'
*The Psalms*

'The privilege of a life-time is to become who you truly are.'

*Carl Jung*

'For what is life but reaching for an answer?'

*Mary Oliver*

'Happiness is elusive, it comes and goes. What we must plant in our inner garden are the seeds of contentment.'

*Rumi*

'Myself it speaks and spells,
crying 'what I do is me: for that I came'

*Gerard Manley Hopkins*

'The whole of religion is like a single tree. Religions are branches and the sects are leaves.'

*Swedenborg*

# INTRODUCTION

'Message for those growing old – you can let go now, let go of what was until now the centre of your life. Leave it behind and start listening to what is inside you. Let go of what has concerned you as an existential being and allow your essential being to manifest itself. Begin to make your way to maturity.'

*Karlfried Durkheim*

# NOVEMBER 2017

## 11 November

Today I reached my 90<sup>th</sup> birthday and there is still so much yet to be discovered. Goethe says 'Become what you are.'

As I look back over my life, I am aware of a long avenue of people who have appeared, often at crucial moments, to point a way forward or to deflect me from some action that would be harmful. And, importantly, there have been those who have not hesitated to hold up a mirror so that I might see clearly my mistakes and my faults – one is indeed blessed if one has friends who are not afraid to speak the truth. I marvel also how many of these encounters seemed almost planned, as though part of an intended pattern. As Joseph Campbell wrote, 'One has only to know and trust and the ageless guardians will appear.'

I recall how at the age of twenty-one, when I was in

a state close to breakdown, I happened to be passing a Catholic church in Ogle Street in London, a church I had never before visited, and being then a devout Catholic, I decided to go in and make my Confession. I never saw the priest, he was just a voice behind a screen, but after listening to me he suggested I make contact with a certain Dr Franz Elkisch in Gloucester Place. And so began the rich years of a Jungian analysis which enabled me to assemble the bits of my own jigsaw, so that I could become the person I was meant to be. Time and again such meetings and encounters have happened.

Lest I seem complacent, all this needs to be set against a background of financial insecurity, some successes, some failures, betrayals, disappointments, doors slamming on one's face – for these, too, are part of the journey and the challenge always is how we deal with setbacks, pain and difficulty.

I have been rereading Cicero on *Old Age*. At one point he says, 'As I approach nearer to death I seem, as it were, to be coming to port at last after a long voyage.' For myself, however many more years I have to live on this earth, I have no fear of dying. How is this? Many decades ago, in a dream, I was shown a boat that looked like a curled leaf. I was told that this was the vessel in which I had come to earth and that in it I would find a return ticket. I knew then that when the time comes I shall indeed return to the place

4

from which I came. It was on telling this dream to Dr Elkisch that he declared, 'Your analysis is now ended'.

I am aware, at this age, of how far I have travelled and yet I am also aware of journeys yet to go, for as T.S.Eliot says in *The Four Quartets*, 'Old men should be explorers still'. And old women also!

Nonetheless I am exhausted. I am uncomfortable with the limelight being turned on me, just because I am 90! However, it has been a happy celebration which began last Sunday when the meditation group assembled, it being the first Sunday in the month, and everyone created a pot luck supper. Piers Plowright made a short speech, but it was very much a family occasion with people forming small groups of two and three to chat, and then we all went into the garden and lit sparklers! But significantly I was in bed twice with a chill, and rose yesterday, on the 10th, feeling groggy, to host a small candlelit dinner at the Garrick Club in the Pinero Room, just fourteen of us.

12 November

Last night I dreamed that I was driving a brand-new model of a vehicle but didn't know how to stop it. Suddenly, in front of me appeared double doors and I shot into a long tunnel which went on and on until it stopped, and I stepped out into the vestibule of a new hotel situated by the sea.

While I waited to fill in forms I could see through a door on my left, at a lower level, a dining room with windows looking out on a beach and the sea far out, the tide not yet having come in, so that there were mud banks and pools of water. There was a single occupant, a young woman, seated at a table, who looked up at me, smiled, then went on eating.

The rushing through the tunnel I interpret as ninety years having rushed past me, so that now I am in a totally different space, the tide not yet in. Here I am to stay a while? To converse with the anima figure and await the turning of the tide?

I am reminded of the nightmare I had a week ago when I woke to hear my lodger knocking on my door, asking if I was all right. I was screaming and kicking violently with my feet, thrusting something away. In the dream my mother was pushing violently at my door, trying to enter. I was kicking at her stomach on the other side of the door. She was very strong. I am aware of the Great Mother archetype who devours her children and crunches up their bones rather than grant them freedom and independence. And I recall my mother, looking at a photograph of me aged six with a mass of Shirley Temple curls (she had hoped for a girl) – 'If only you had stayed like that!' she said. In fact a few days before she died, she told me, sitting up in bed, 'Thank you, darling for everything. You couldn't have done better had you been a girl.' To which I replied, 'What a thing to say to a man of fifty!'

## 13 November

In bed with this chill.

## 14 November

Jonathan, my doctor, arrives on a house visit. For the somewhat chronic pain on the left of my waist, he is arranging an x-ray – it could be to do with the colon.

## 15 November

In bed, groggy with cold, nose streaming. Yesterday afternoon was traumatic as a friend discovered I was being cheated of nearly £5000 on my visa card. I am stunned and bewildered. It took an hour on the phone here, then a taxi to the nearest Nat West in the Finchley Road, our local branch having been closed down, and then he spent another two hours sorting it all out. I couldn't have done it without him. But now I have lost my wallet!! The fragility of age!

## 16 November

I rally to go and teach my American students.

## 18 November

When I give recitals with the harpist Frances Kelly, I call the programme *The Journey Thus Far*, as the readings, both poetry and prose, are from those passages that have most influenced me through my own journey, but I always make one point about ageing: that when people say 'I am old' I reply, 'no, you are older!' The word 'old' with its final 'd' is like the thudding sound of a door closing – life is over. We are older, yes, but still learning, still growing, right up to the very end.

## 19 November

I have been rereading a letter from a musician friend, who is married with grown up children. She writes, 'I have had a very busy few months where all the work came at once, and I fear I was too tired to give it my best at times.

'It's a strange place, this being in your 6Os. Some work is tailing off as new generations get together, new groups are being formed. I take delight in seeing students I have taught making their way successfully in the profession; at the same time it's hard to let go, and there is still pressure (and necessity) to earn a living! There is an ageism there, and also, and I hate to say it, a certain sexism... but also there are two undeniable realities: firstly, that I no longer have the energy, concentration and stamina of a few years back, and my musical memory which has always been so stalwart is no longer quick nor as reliable. Secondly, I do feel it's important to let the young ones in – they need their chance and we shouldn't hold on for dear life.

'Oh dear! If I were an athlete, dancer – or even a singer, I would have had to face up to this long ago... still, you are an inspiration, and on the whole I accept the change. I am aware sometimes I want to lay down tools and give up, and I'm not a born fighter... but making music is such an important part of my whole being. Still, I trust the right way will emerge.'

The point here is that each decade calls for subtle, sometimes major, changes. And we have to learn how to be open to change. Also, it can happen that the real purpose of our life often only manifests itself midway. As in the story of Barbara Robb, the wife of Brian Robb, the artist who illustrated all seven of my children's books, *The Adventures of Odd and Elsewhere*.

Barbara, as a young woman, trained as a ballet dancer until she damaged a foot, which caused her to have to give up her incipient career. She then trained as an artist, and later, having had analysis, she became an art therapist. However, it was not until she was in her fifties that her real life's work was revealed when she discovered that her old nanny was in hospital, in a ward where forty beds were crammed together, the geriatric patients stripped of their spectacles, dentures, hearing aids and other civilised necessities, leaving them to vegetate in utter loneliness and idleness. This was the case not only in mental hospitals but many other hospitals. Tens of thousands of old people at that time were still in mental hospitals. And this Dickensian situation was in the affluent 1960s! It took her several months to get her old nanny moved to a private home. She then set out to travel the country, talking with doctors and nurses in hospitals for the elderly, and produced a book entitled *Sans Everything*, which sold out on publication and was serialised in *The Observer*. In October 1965, with the help of Lord Strabolgi, she formed the AEGIS Group. This had three aims: to make the public aware of certain very serious defects that existed in the care of many of the government's elderly patients, to devise and propagate remedies for these, and to encourage the use of modern methods of geriatric care, with their strong emphasis on rehabilitation. As a result major changes were brought about in Parliament so that such conditions would never exist again.

## 20 NOVEMBER

I have been much influenced in my life by the writings of Joseph Campbell. His most famous phrase is perhaps 'Follow your bliss', which does not mean one should be self-indulgent, and to hell with everyone else, but finding out what kind of person you are meant to be. 'Move, move, move into the Transcendent!' he says in one of his talks. 'Get rid of the life you have planned in order to have the life that's waiting to be yours.' I know that this why Mary Oliver's poem 'The Journey', which I teach each year to my American students, is so meaningful to them. They know the pressures from parents, teachers, and society (perhaps even more so in the extrovert culture of America), of having to be successful, to make a lot of money.

The poem begins with the words:

'One day you finally knew
what you had to do, and began...'

And in breaking away the poet begins to hear a new voice which she slowly recognises as her own, that keeps her company as she strides deeper and deeper into the world, 'determined to do the only thing you could do – determined to save the only life you could save.'

I am reminded of one of the most contented men I ever knew, Neville Dewis. He was the resident stage designer at the Salisbury Playhouse in the 1970s. Then one day, seated on a hilltop, he thought – do I want to go on churning out stage designs every three weeks for the rest of my life? It was then that the word 'soil' came into his head. He gave up his job at the theatre, bought a bicycle and became a jobbing gardener for about fourteen houses. He lived in a rented cottage, one of a row, in Bretherton, opposite the Rectory where George Herbert had been Rector. He grew his own vegetables and was able to rent one room to visiting actors and directors, which is how I came to know him when directing the world première of *84 Charing Cross Road* in 1981. At that time he averagely earned the modest sum of £100 a week.

Many people, especially men, in their forties, experience a mid-life crisis, realising that something essential is missing from their lives. But it is never too late to change direction.

## 21 NOVEMBER

A day of clearing. I have been stacking in the centre of the room all the archival material, including fifty years of my journals, which is going to the Harry Ransome archives in Austin Texas... All my life I have collected, documented, archived, and now in these last years I am happy to let it all go, to shed it. This is another important lesson as one grows older, the willingness to let go, of things and of people... as when friends die. Truly one can say we brought nothing into this world and we take nothing from it! The aim is to travel lightly, knowing that we are here for but a short time before we move on.

## 22 November

I sleep heavily till noon! And am quite dizzy and uncertain on my feet.

## 23 November

An interesting sign of age is my frustration with inanimate objects, which cause me to swear! Sometimes when I drop something, or my foot gets caught in the sheet when getting out of bed, I growl, 'Fuck the bloody sheet!' or trying to put on my socks, the left foot is easy but putting a sock on the right foot is much more of an effort!

## 24 November

Guests to lunch. Because my right ear has an infection I can't wear my hearing aid in that ear, so I can't always follow what's being said.

## 25 November

I noted some days ago my delight in letting go of possessions. I am also letting go of other things. For instance, I am declining all invitations to lunch or dinner, as I find these quite a strain, though I am happy to welcome people here. I have also decided not to review any more books, and I watch very little television. This withdrawal is not, however, as negative as it might seem: it is more a centring down, and I see it as a positive action.

It is interesting to read what the conductor Sir Colin Davis, who was born the same year as myself, had to say about being in his eighties:

'One's ego becomes less and less interesting as you get older, to oneself and to everyone else. I have been around it too long. The less ego you have the more influence you have as a conductor.'

*The Guardian, 12 May 2011*

26 NOVEMBER

Old age presents the challenge of making sense of what has been, in the knowledge of what is to come. For so many today, however, retirement means not only loss of work, but also loss of identity, and loss of income. According to a recent report in 2012 by the Alzheimer's Society, 50 per cent of people aged 75 and over live alone; while about 5 million older people say that television is their main source of company. People feel they no longer have a part to play, while partners die, and children move away. This is why the work of the Baring Foundation is so important in encouraging creative opportunities for older people in the arts, from painting to singing, dancing to acting, so that for many there is a profound transformation from social passivity to creativity and fulfilment. As Francois Matarasso observes in his book, *Winter Fires*, 'By simply pursuing their artistic interests in their seventies, eighties and nineties, the present generation is inevitably changing what it means to be old, transforming a state that has been characterised by social passivity into one that is animated and active. They are rewriting the story of ageing and the consequences will be important for their children and their children's children.'

And the importance of encouraging creativity in others has been central to the work of the Bleddfa Trust, which I founded in 1974, in Radnorshire. In the Barn Centre at Bleddfa there are some words by the Spanish poet, Federico Garcia Lorca, which sum up what Bleddfa stands for:

> The poem, the song, the picture,
> is only water
> drawn from the well of the people
> and it should be given back to them in a cup of
> beauty
> so that they may drink
> and in drinking understand themselves.'

As Bleddfa's chief patron, the Most Rev. Dr Rowan

Williams has said, 'It is by encouraging creative expression in everyone that we help them to become fully human.'

The tragedy of so many lives is that suddenly, and often too late, people are aware of having wasted their lives, of never having fulfilled their potential: born millionaires, they die in poverty. The relationship between creativity and spirituality is something that is still little understood. By spirituality I mean the development of a person's innermost self. Sadly, as Joanna Trollope observed in her novel, *The Rector's Wife*, 'so many people lack the capacity to live life richly at any level.'

What is important to realise is that most people possess, no matter how unused, real creative and imaginative faculties. People need to discover, or rediscover, how to give form to their most urgent feelings, conflicts, yearnings and joys, so that they may the better understand themselves and others. There is a line in the Psalms, 'With the harp I will solve my problem'. Making music, being in a choir, keeping a journal, gardening, all these are ways of growing in understanding.

Our task must be to enable people to exercise their own creativity in whatever form: through movement, dance, sound, music, belonging to a quilting group, or making music with others. Above all to learn that it is in their living, in their loving – whether in the creation of a relationship, a home or a garden, for we are all capable in some form or other of being artists. In art, as in love, we give ourselves. There are, for instance, some homes and some relationships that, when you walk into them, you are immediately aware of something created with the discipline of love.

We all know how much more meaningful it is to be given something that another person has made rather than bought from an expensive boutique: a loaf of bread, a cake, a hand-knitted scarf, a plant grown from seed, a basket of vegetables from someone's garden, an unexpected meal, or a warm embrace. Love is the basis of it all. As Jeannette Winterston once remarked in an interview with Bel Mooney, 'My work in this world is to open people up to the joy and the strength that is in life and in themselves. And to get people out of this littleness, this feeling of being bound in, this feeling of being out of control. One of the reasons I am so passionate about art is because it is so large and because it opens cathedrals in the mind where you can go and be and you can pray and you are not small. We have to be able to put meaning back into the lives of people.'

## 27 November

I think often of Sean Dunne, the Irish poet and writer, aged 38, who having kissed his two small boys good-night, climbed into bed with his wife, and when she woke the next morning he was dead. None of us knows the hour when death will eventually claim us, but as we reach our eighties it is more natural to become aware that we are approaching the end of our journey. Like Longfellow we realise that for all our achievements and honours, small or great, we 'leave behind us, footsteps in the sands of time,' footprints which will be erased by the next tide. With Virgil we are aware that 'irretrievable time is flying'.

In his book *The Tibetan Book of Living and Dying*, Sogyal Rinpoche describes how, when he first came to the West in 1970, what disturbed him most was the almost complete lack of spiritual help for the dying. He had been told many stories of people dying alone and in great distress and disillusion, many without any spiritual help, any guidance. Wherever he went he was struck by the great mental suffering that arises from the fear of dying, whether or not this fear is acknowledged. In Tibet it was a natural response to pray for the dying, and to give them spiritual care. In the West the only spiritual attention that most people pay to the dying is to go to their funeral. At the moment of their greatest vulnerability, he remarked, people are abandoned and left almost totally without support or insight.

But what is this fear of dying? Is it not compounded of all our fears? The fear of failure, the fear that love will not last and that in the end we shall be rejected, and left alone; the fear that we may lose our job and not be able to pay the rent or our mortgage, and other bills; the fear that we have taken on too much, that we are too much the high flyer; the fear that we may do something irrational that will ruin our lives or our careers. We think we are in control of our lives until, suddenly, something takes hold of us and sends us sprawling. In addition there are atavistic fears, far more common than we realise or care to admit, such as fear of the dark, of the unexpected, of small animals and insects. Some live in terror of being mugged, or of being stranded in an unknown place. Many of these fears are projections of our shadow side; those aspects of our natures that all too often we prefer to ignore and even deny that they exist. A fear of heights may be traced back to a childhood experience. Similarly early experiences of family break up, of incest and abuse, early betrayal by an authority figure, whether parent, priest, teacher or relative; sexual fears and failures... the list is endless and, however mature or successful we may become, all too often these fears lie just beneath the surface, waiting for an opportunity to manifest themselves.

But what do all these fears have in common? Is it not the fear of the unknown, typified by fear of the dark when nothing can be identified, when all orientation is lost? It is the fear of not knowing our identity. Who am I really? It is in this sense that, throughout our lives, we experience many small deaths on the way to physical death.

But what lies beyond death? – 'The undiscovered country from whose bourn no traveller returns'. For myself I have no fear of dying and at a deep intuitive level I know that there is a continuity. D.H. Lawrence, as he lay dying in the south of France wrote,

'Build your ship of death... for the longest voyage of all'.

## 28 NOVEMBER

Jonathan, my doctor, rang – I have to be at the surgery for a blood test at 11 15, prior to the x-ray of my stomach tomorrow, and at 11 30 I see a doctor about the ear infection, which is ever so painful and not responding to drops. Then on to lunch at the Garrick with Malcolm Johnson, a priest friend who on email always addresses me as 'Owlie', as he thinks I am a wise one! I don't think I am, certainly not as wise and perceptive as my lodger, who at 38, has remarkable insights into people. What I am good at is being a listener, although it has often got me into trouble with women! I recall one woman friend saying sharply to me, 'You must stop looking at women the way you do!' She wouldn't explain and I was very puzzled. At the time I was directing Annie Rogers as Blanche in *A Streetcar Named Desire* and I told her. 'It's obvious!' she said. 'You listen so intently and women, in the main, aren't used to a man listening to them so totally, and then of course they think you are in love with them!'

Listening is an art and I recall my favourite story about Brother Gregory. He was a Franciscan friar at Glasshampton Monastery in Worcestershire. He told me how the headmaster of a top school, either Harrow or Eton, asked him if he would see a sixteen-year-old boy, from a very good family, who was heavily into drugs. Gregory saw the boy and then, a few weeks later, had a letter from the headmaster saying, 'I don't know what you said to the boy but he is totally changed.'

'The funny thing is,' said Brother Gregory to me, 'I didn't say anything. I just listened.' But clearly such was the quality of his listening that the boy, in talking about his problems, saw himself as in a mirror.

29 NOVEMBER

Today I go to the Royal Free Hospital for an x-ray of my stomach and colon to try and find what is causing this pain in my side.

I continue to reflect on the latter end of this life. Death, as Swedenborg taught, is but a transition from one state to another. We die but to be reborn. As John O'Donohue observed, 'When we see someone dying, that is what we see. But to those waiting on the other side, they are watching someone being born.'

How we go through that final door, how we die,

will depend upon how we respond to the many hourly, daily, yearly experiences of dying that we encounter in our lives. If we learn how to live through each of these smaller deaths then each can become a resurrection, every ending a new beginning. And if, as we journey down the years, we do this, then we shall also hear, increasingly nearer, that music from another room which is the life beyond and yet is all about us even now. As Edith Sitwell wrote, 'Love is not changed by death. And nothing is lost, and all in the end is harvest.'

Today I fasted until 11 30 when I arrived at the Royal Free Hospital for a stomach x-ray timed for 11 45. It is an hour and half before I am called, but I observe how crowded this large hospital is with sick people of all ages and races, and how the staff are fully stretched. I shall be there again on Friday when I have a colonoscopy under sedation to see what is going in the area of my colon, which aches all the time and is prone to giving sharp stabs of pain.

30 NOVEMBER

The pain in my ear is so excruciating, and worse at night when it throbs, that at 6 30 this evening I will see an ear specialist privately at the St John and St Elizabeth, rather than wait until Tuesday to see an NHS specialist.

Mr D'Souza, the ear specialist at the St John and St Elizabeth, syringed my ear, a painful process, but he got out all the muck, and refused to charge a fee, so all I have to pay is the hospital fee. The lodger, back from teaching in Berkshire, urges me not to go out for the next few days, as there is frost and snow, though I have to fast tomorrow until 2 p.m. when I go for my endoscopy examination, and my friend Tusse will see me home in a cab.

# DECEMBER 2017

## 2 December

The lodger leaves for several days to visit his mother, his brother and friends. Charlie comes at 11 to talk about the break up of his marriage after more than thirty years. His wife won't speak, won't open up, but insists they separate, and so the house is up for sale.

I am still under the weather so I have cancelled Stefan coming to lunch on Wednesday, Charlie on Thursday, and Gill on Saturday. I plan to take the week quietly which the lodger has been counselling – sometimes I am stubborn, but I am learning! The great blessing of having younger friends is that they don't stand on ceremony but speak bluntly.

## 4 December

I don't know what happened with today – for it has gone! It is partly that my ear infection has been so throbbingly painful. I was unable to get to sleep until about 5 a.m., and only then by taking a painkiller.

## 5 December

I have just discovered among many papers the following from John O'Donohue:

> 'When you are understood, you are at home… a friend is a loved one who awakens your life to free the wild possibilities within you.'

Of course there is a great difference between loving someone and being in love. To love someone is to draw close to that person as a human being, whereas being in love is to make a divinity out of that person which they cannot live up to! As James Hollis observes in his excellent book *The Middle Passage*, 'Living together on a daily basis wears away the projections, and one is left with the otherness of the Other,' so that couples often end up saying 'You're not the person I married' but they never were! Each has to go on growing as an individual within the container of the relationship. A marriage or a partnership is only as good as the two people in it.

## 6 December

Still suffering from a chill and the ear throbbing, but about 6 30 Chris drops by and we share a bottle of white wine. Though so young – 33, I learn much from him.

## 7 December

The past two weeks I have been coping with a throbbing and deeply painful ear infection, and am generally low, so I am quite glad that the lodger has been away. There are times when it is better to work through such physical setbacks on one's own, but he returns late tonight, when I shall be fast asleep, but his return makes me also very happy! He is someone very special in my life. When my partner of 54 years died five years ago I was content to be on my own and besides I could not imagine sharing this space with anyone else. So for three years I was here on my own. Then a friend gave a copy of my book on meditation, *Finding Silence*, to a young colleague who, he told me, was reading it daily in the bath! I was so intrigued I said let us meet. He then came to various meals when always he would ask me questions about Hywel, trying to build up a picture of him, which I found deeply healing. Most of our friends obviously had known Hywel, and those who hadn't were too shy to ask. Finally I said would he like to live here, having his own room and bathroom, and that it would be like a Brotherhood of Two: one elderly monk and one younger: an entirely platonic friendship.

Living with such a person, who has his own life and circle of friends, has proved richly challenging, and each day I find myself learning new things, new attitudes.

## 8 DECEMBER

The pain in my right ear, which has been there for two weeks, and does not seem to be responding to treatment, is so intense and throbbing, I have never known anything like it. But it is good nonetheless to have this experience, to know a little of what some people have to endure. I make an appointment to see Mr D'Souza again on Monday at the London Bridge Hospital this time.

## 9 DECEMBER

... Lying awake till five in the morning, such throbbing pain. In the end I risk taking two Ibuprofen, and fall into a deep sleep till 11 30. This morning the pain seems less, so maybe something is working.

I am reminded of some words of Henry James: 'Observe. Observe. Observe the onslaught of old age.' In other words not to be self-pitying, or burden one's friends with organ recitals but to view dispassionately what is happening.

I am aware, for instance, that my balance is not what it once was and that I feel safer, when out walking, if I have my shopping trolley with me. When I am at the Garrick Club for a meal and I get up to go to the toilet, I am aware that my walk is that of an old man. I am reminded of a marvellous passage from the autobiography of Augustus Hare:

'Every morning when I am in London I work at the Athenaeum, less disturbed there even than here. There is no place where Death makes a stranger impression than at the Athenaeum. You become so accustomed to many men you do not know, to their comings and goings, that they become almost part of your daily life. You watch them growing older; the dapper young man becoming grizzled, first too careful and then too neglectful of his dress; you see his face become furrowed, his hair grow grey and then white, and at last he is lame and bent. You become worried by his coughs and hems and little peculiarities. And suddenly you are aware that he is not there, and all your little annoyances immediately seem to have been absurd. For a time you miss him; he never comes. He will cough no more; no longer creak across the floor. He has passed into the unseen; gradually he is forgotten.

His place knows him no more. But the wheel goes on turning; it is for others; it is for one's self, perhaps, who is waning away.'

## 10 DECEMBER

I set the alarm for eight o'clock, but the Ibuprofen causes me to sleep so deeply that I never hear the telephone, which rings for about 20 minutes and finally wakes up the lodger who then wakes me up! Rupert Shortt is coming to breakfast at 9 30, after Mass at St Dominic's. I quickly bathe and start to prepare the breakfast when I see, out of the window, everything mantled in white, and the snow falling steadily. And then there comes a message on my laptop from Rupert saying he had set out in his car but had to turn back.

## 11 DECEMBER

To lunch with Jeffrey Martin, head of Drama at the Roger Williams University for which every Fall I have taught an acting course for the past 46 years, and Jane Passes, of Scholar Services who organises those courses. I have decided that the time has come to stop teaching.

## 12 December

Last night I saw Mr d'Souza, this time at the Shard at London Bridge. Again he refused to charge, saying 'my colleagues don't always understand me. Of course I have to make money but I didn't come into medicine just to do that. And so I continue with not charging some patients.' I leave him an inscribed copy of my memoirs.

When I return it is to find no hot water and no lights at all in the conservatory area, and we are mystified. I call Mariusz and, like a guardian angel, he appears about an hour later to sort out the problem!

A friend emails me 'the older I get the more I realise I have to face up to all the filth in me if I am to reach the end at peace with myself.' This, I think, is an important aspect of reaching a ripe age, perhaps any age, that we become aware of, and accept, our many failures and shortcomings. There are those with whom one has been too brusque or pushed to one side in one's ruthless pursuit of success; there have been the petty lies and betrayals in relationships, the sexual infidelities, and sometimes much more serious acts of betrayal, or causing unnecessary pain. We have to acknowledge our failures, our weaknesses and our insensitivity towards others in the same way that we acknowledge the many good acts we have performed. We have to see ourselves in the whole.

In some ways one of the most important aspects of meditation is the way that all sorts of filth rise to the surface: hidden angers, jealousies, resentments, lust. We have to learn how to accept all these negative things within us and, like Prospero in *The Tempest*, speaking of the demi-devil Caliban, be able to say 'This thing of darkness I acknowledge as mine,' rather like a person in analysis.

The bottom line is that we each have to take responsibility for ourselves. The only person you can change is ourself.

### 13 December

The pain in the ear and skull is such that I ring the specialist's secretary and make an appointment for a scan at the St John and St Elizabeth tomorrow. It is difficult to eat. All very boring.

### 14 December

Reflecting on the dependence of the present generation on their iPads, mobiles, computers – some have the radio or television on all day; some even take their iPhones to bed! What is this fear of silence? What is it? The dependency on technology is surely an admission of loneliness, the need to be needed, and so long as Facebook and Twitter exist, we are not alone. Yet silence is the gateway to a deeper richness and is a necessary part of the journey to be taken alone. Perhaps this explains why also the practice of meditation by a group is both powerful and helpful, when one shares this deeper silence with others. No words are needed but we are bonded by the silence even while each person's meditation is different.

Although I have had several major operations in my life I have never known pain such as I am experiencing now with this ear infection. What my experience of pain has enabled me to understand is why some should choose to end their lives rather than live with such intensive pain.

Back from seeing Mr d'Souza. The inflammation is less, he says and he has given me some very powerful painkillers that are already working, to my great relief.

I have received an email from a student I met in America in the 1970s, who has been married twice, worked for the American government, is now retired and spends his days playing golf. How many such men, on retiring, play golf if they have the means, or spend hours in the betting shop, or simply slump in front of the television. Women, however, are better at adjusting to the changing decades. We have one life and each of us should live it as fully as possible, and that means living it for others.

15 DECEMBER

A lively dinner party here. And afterwards everyone reads a poem.

## 17 December

I have been reflecting on relationships and what I may have learned over the course of the years. Loving has to be worked at. It is no wonder that Rilke, writing to a young poet, says 'It is good to love because love is difficult. For one human being to love another is perhaps the most difficult task that has been entrusted to us, the ultimate task, the final test and proof, the work for which all other work is a preparation. This is why young people, who are beginners in everything, are not yet capable of love: it is something they must learn. With their whole being, with all their forces, they must learn to love.'

This means often that the first love affair often fails, yet, if one can learn from the mistakes made, then the second has a greater chance of succeeding. What is important is not to niggle over small differences but when there is a major clash, not to be emotional, but quietly to talk through whatever is the problem in order to arrive at a solution, seeking a resolution. We are all imperfect beings! And the journey of discovery continues to the very end.

## 18 December

I have been prescribed stronger painkillers plus a course of antibiotics, which meant I had several hours of deep sleep after all these weeks. But the throbbing continues, especially when I lie down. I may have to have a small operation.

## 19 DECEMBER

In the December issue of the Garrick Club's newsletter I read about Sir Maurice Bowra's parody of John Betjeman's 'In Westminster Abbey', which he composed after seeing the poet collect a literary award from Princess Margaret:

> 'Green with lust and sick with shyness,
> Let me lick your lacquered toes.
> Gosh, oh gosh, your Royal Highness,
> Put your finger up my nose'.

Reading that, I recall how when I was up at Oxford and Maurice Bowra was Vice-Chancellor, he used to bathe in the nude with other dons at what was called Parson's Pleasure. One day some women passed by and all the dons immediately put their hands in front of their genitals, except for Maurice Bowra who placed his over his face!

## 20 DECEMBER, 3 28 A.M.!

With major dreams it is important not to try and solve them like a crossword puzzle but, like an egg, allow them time to hatch. Slowly the life within the dream stirs, and eventually cracks the shell, and emerges. A new insight is born. And so now I have at this early hour woken with a deeper insight into the end of the dream in which my 90 years flashed by in an instant, bringing me to a place of quiet. This is a newly built hotel by the sea, right on the beach, full of light and space. The only other occupant is this young woman seated in the dining room, which is down some steps, on a lower level than the reception area where I am checking in. Without question she represents my *anima* but, interestingly, is not a wise old woman but young and full of life, sparkling with energy and clarity of insight. I note also that the tide is far out and so the time for sailing on the next stage of my journey is not yet.

What does this signify, especially her youth?

This young woman represents new life, the beginning of a new journey. It is clear from what I have written elsewhere that I know that this life is not the only one, but that beyond death is a new birth, a new existence, a continuing growth. This cannot be proved scientifically but in the deepest part of me 'I know'.

21 DECEMBER

Ultimately each of us is alone. This is an existential fact. We often protect ourselves against this by sharing our life with a partner but with the death of the one closest to us we are thrust back on ourselves. As one friend wrote to me, 'When you lose the one you love, the rest of your life is like a journey on a long road where you might be ambushed at any time, around any corner, as in the old days of highwaymen. Now it is tears that come from nowhere and you have to pick yourself up again and smile, and drive on to the end.'

We often don't realise how some people give us purpose in life until we lose them. And yet we have to learn how to let go – not of love, for that endures – we have to learn to stand on our own feet, and that takes time and skill.

None of us owns anything, let alone another human being. But for a time we are entrusted to one another. It is important to travel lightly.

## 22 December

I am back from the ENT Hospital, where both ears were syringed. I gripped the edge of the bed because of the pain; I wouldn't have survived one minute on the Inquisition's rack! I return next Friday but have been given different drops to put in.

## 23 December

I have been thinking more about relationships and how when two people choose to live together bits of the ego keep being chipped off in the process. But for some individuals, who have lived alone until middle age and then form a relationship, it isn't going to be easy for the other partner, as the first one will be set in their ways and friction can arise. 'Why do you always do this or that?' and the answer comes, 'Because I always have!'

I recall reading an article about living in a monastic community, which was likened to a leather bag filled with small stones that, over time, as they get knocked around, slowly become smooth. And even in a community of two people – perhaps even more so – this is true.

It is helpful to recall what Jung has to say about marriage (and that today also includes civil partnership). Marriage, he says, as a sacred institution, is to be understood as a special form of individuation. 'One of the essential features is the absence of avenues of escape. Just as the saintly hermits cannot evade themselves, so the married persons cannot escape their partners.' Jung, like Erich Fromm and others, emphasises that a true and lasting bond between two people demands a growing recognition by each partner as an individual, learning to love the other for being the person they happen to be, warts and all!

Prophecy Coles has just sent me a copy of her latest book, *Psychological and Psychotherapeutic Perspectives on Stepfamilies and Step-parenting*, and what is disturbing, in terms of human relationships, is the fact that today we live in a society where almost half of our children come from divorced families. 'It is a painful fact but all the research evidence suggests these children are emotionally hurt by divorce. The contentious issue is whether this damage can be healed well enough so the wound does not open up again when adult life proves difficult. I have come to the conclusion that it would be a mistake to think that "divorce is a transient crisis" and that children will recover from trauma. They are changed for life, though, yes, some may survive better than others.'

Prophecy also produces the evidence that the divorce rate of a first marriage today is well over 50 per cent and most frequently occurs between the fourth and eighth year of marriage. Elsewhere she makes the observation that while divorce can liberate adults it can also inflict a wound upon a child's trust, a wound that can remain open, and fester, for life.

## 24 December, Christmas Eve

I have covered the low table in front of the sofa with ivy and holly and in the centre, on a white cloth, I have placed the image of a newborn male child.

Someone with whom I correspond almost daily asks if I celebrate Christmas in any special way. I no longer feel the need to go to church. This is not to say that going to church (the temple or the synagogue) is wrong, far from it, but I have moved on now, and no longer feel such a need. And whether Jesus was born in Bethlehem or Nazareth, or at this time of year, is no longer relevant. What one celebrates is the birth of a new teacher, bringing light into the darkness, assuring us that there is a world – or even worlds – beyond this one.

What matters is the phrase of Meister Eckhart that 'God is waiting eternally to be born in each of us.' Such a thought transcends all religions. We celebrate the birth of 'meaning' in our lives, the recognition that each of us has a specific purpose for being here.

I have been reflecting how deep down in all of us there is a loneliness, a need to be embraced, hugged, held, acknowledged for one's true self. The merest touch of a hand or a kiss. And between two lovers, at the climax of lovemaking the two become one in an oceanic bliss. One achieves, for a brief moment, true contentment in the act of holding and being held. As Sir Philip Sydney wrote:

'My true love has my heart and I have his,
By just exchange one for the other given.'

An embrace is a reaching out with the heart, like a wave flowing in to shore, or a bird flying home at dusk to roost, or the sudden glow of embers in a fire. A true embrace reaches out to enfold another human being, yet never seeks to possess. Our arms reach out to enfold and then they open again to release the one who is embraced. I recall how at the age of 18, doing my National Service, and stationed in Trieste, I was received into the Catholic Church. After my First Communion in the packed local church the priest stood with me on the steps outside and said, 'E contento adesso?' It is difficult to translate that word as it meant on that occasion so much more than simple contentment: it also implied being fulfilled, coming home, being held in a great love. For me the Eucharist was indeed the food of love.

## 25 DECEMBER, CHRISTMAS DAY, 3 A.M.

Because I wake several times in the night to have a pee, I am almost always conscious of a great deal of dream activity which vanishes with the swiftness of a conjuring trick or melting snow. The unconscious is sorting through the day's experiences, like someone sorting through rubbish, but every now and then, one comes across something important. That becomes the dream one remembers. Some dreams yield up their meaning instantly but many are like riddles, Sphinx-like, and have to be meditated on.

10.45 I am already bathed and in my new pyjamas when the lodger taps on my door to say 'Happy Christmas' and I join him in front of the fire where he has set out glasses of fruit juice, coffee, croissants and other delights. We then proceed to open our stockings. His gifts to me are practical: an alarm clock, an instrument for getting juice out of a lemon, as well as two books, one being a novel based on the Dreyfus story by Robert Harris.

For decades in Wales, in front of a real fire of logs and coal, Hywel and I, and any friends staying, would sit and open our gifts at 11 a.m. – the world absolutely quiet, wrapped in snow. This morning the lodger and I sat before the artificial fire flickering in the grate, and although there was no snow, it was so quiet.

In the evening he cooked a festive meal of crown of turkey, with all the trappings, for us two and Chris. I stay up late, unable to put down the Robert Harris book! The lodger stays in the centre room, lying on the sofa, reading articles on his iPhone and then listening to Bach, while I read. Usually he comes in just for five or ten minutes and then out again. This sharing made me very happy.

## 26 December

Dan to supper, and we each have to name and then listen to two pieces of our favourite music. I choose the slow movement of Beethoven's Violin Concerto, which I first heard on the radio when I was 14, and then Arvo Part's Spiegel im Spiegel. The lodger chooses the glorious 'Wachet Auf' chorus, which I shall ask to be played at my funeral as the coffin is carried down the church at the end. It is all about going to the marriage feast.

## 27 DECEMBER

9 15 this morning. I wake to hear knocking on the door and it was my lodger alerting me to the fact that the alarm clock was ringing and I hadn't heard it.

I fall back into a deep sleep and don't wake till noon. I think all this socialising is quite tiring at my age, or perhaps simply that because of the continuing pain in the ear I can only use one hearing aid. Often I miss key words and have to ask 'What did you say?' Very boring for everyone.

## 28 DECEMBER

Norman is coming to supper tonight. He wanted to take me out but I am not keen on noisy restaurants. The ear is somewhat calmer and tomorrow I go to the ENT in Gray's Inn Road. Anthony calls for coffee, bringing gifts of rare cheese from Fortnum's plus special chutney and croissants. He had cancer of the throat and now has a box so that in order to speak he has to keep a finger at his throat. He follows my blog and says the one that most moved him was the one about how each of us has a guardian angel.

## 29 DECEMBER

I woke to hear the new alarm clock not only ringing but in its vibration falling off the bedside table.

I am just back from four hours at the ENT hospital in Gray's Inn Road – a skeletal staff and many patients, so much patient waiting...

## 30 DECEMBER

Tony, who is a barrister, comes for dinner.

## 31 DECEMBER

Thinking about the need for rituals, for so many life experiences, I am reminded how in my book *Passages of the Soul: Ritual Today*, I remarked how time and again we lack rituals which can mark and celebrate key moments in our lives. We have no rituals for a woman who has been raped, beaten or battered. No rituals for parents who have had to experience an abortion, a miscarriage or a stillborn child. There are no rituals for pregnancy, none for a broken marriage, a broken relationship or a broken home. What rituals do we have for a child moving to a new school or a new neighbourhood? What rituals exist for a young woman's first menstruation or a boy coming to puberty? What rituals do we have for the elders of our society – why do we wait until someone is dead before we say how much we valued them? And while each of the major faiths has precise rituals for the dying and the dead, what rituals do we have to offer to those of no specific faith or tradition?

What so many do not realise is that there is a pattern and a purpose that makes each life different and, therefore, unique.

Dorothy Duffy tells me how when she was living in a cottage in Donegal, one day, while she was getting in the coal, a beautiful black dog appeared out of nowhere, alone. She had no idea where the dog had come from and she never saw it again. Her first reaction was that the dog must be lost, so she went over to pet it and saw a collar round its neck with a little tag that read, 'I'm not lost. I just like to explore.' That, said Dorothy, 'was one of the most powerful messages I have ever received. I always had the feeling that I was lost but in truth I was always exploring.'

# JANUARY 2018

## 1 JANUARY

It is now 9 30 and as I am preparing to withdraw the
lodger says, 'You're not going to bed, are you? You slept
till midday!' and then he adds, 'You're not depressed
are you?' and I reply, no. But, like many older people,
I find the dark winter nights difficult. But I must not
withdraw too much. I can see how easy it would be. I
am blessed not only with him as a close friend, sharing
this flat, but also in having so many devoted friends. So
many elderly people today live alone.

## 2 JANUARY

I realise that, unerringly, the lodger has put his finger
on the reason why I retreat to my bed so early in the
evening. 'Are you depressed?' he asked, and I told him

no, of course. But I realise that deep down I still ache from the loss of Hywel, my partner in my life, who at so many levels was central to my being.

All our loves tend towards union; they are the central forces in our lives. Yet in such a love there is no narcissism, for each completes the other. As Joseph Campbell wrote, 'in marriage or a committed relationship each partner works to enable the other to become their full self.' Through interaction, sometimes painful, Hywel and I each grew as individuals. There are so many photographs of us both at the gate of our Welsh home either greeting friends on arrival or waving them goodbye. Each home we made was a reflection of our two selves.

And so bereavement means that one is thrown back on one's self and one has to work at rebuilding one's inner self. Some, sadly, never achieve this, finding the process too painful. When Hywel died, what helped was not only many years of good analysis, but also the practice of meditation. Learning to let go seems such an important precept as we age. Letting go of things, the accumulation of possessions, simplifying, letting light into dark corners, and clearing space for new growth.

3 JANUARY

The lodger rings to ask would I like venison sausages and mash for supper tonight? Yes, please, I reply.

My friend Jenny Pearson, who set up the first week

long Story-Telling workshop at Bleddfa, which is now an annual event, writes to tell me how much she enjoys the paintings of the late Kyffin Willams, who spent his latter years living in Anglesey and became a friend of the Angleseys. I tell her how when I used to stay with Henry and Shirley Anglesey at Plas Newydd there were a series of caricatures in the guest bathroom, each with a verse written by Kyffin Williams. The one that I loved was of a very recognisable face, and then these words:

I met a man I can't think where
Who said that he was Tony Blair
But what was really odd
He also said that he was God!

It reminded me of when Rowan Williams came to Bleddfa to give the annual Bleddfa Lecture, as Archbishop of Canterbury, and at the luncheon afterwards, one of the guests, Dr Andrew Elder, asked Rowan what he thought of Tony Blair. 'He's very strong on God,' was the reply, and then he paused, before adding, 'but weak on irony!'

A lasting memory of Plas Newydd, where I stayed often, either on my own or with Hywel, is of one evening in the kitchen when an altercation broke out between Shirley and Henry. 'Henry, I believe you have given the National Trust permission to floodlight the front of the house at night?'

'That's right, Mother,' he replied.

'Henry, I cannot bear the thought that every time I go into my room I will have to draw the curtains!'

'Calm down, Mother!' replied Henry. The conversation got so heated that I quietly slipped away to my room. A little later I hear the thud, thud of Henry's heavy boots tramping along the passage, then the clang of the gates of the lift as he descended to his study on the ground floor with its seven desks.

A little later there was a tap on my door. It was Shirley Anglesey. 'You can come out now,' she smiled, 'I've won.'

I also remember asking how Henry proposed to her. It was wartime and he drove her up to Plas Newydd for the first time, and on the upper floor, opened the shutters – revealing Snowdon in the moonlight. And that was the moment, said Shirley, he proposed.

4 JANUARY

Into town to buy new sandals and a pair of slippers. The wind was so strong it blew off my beret and then, suddenly, a violent gust nearly knocked me over. I recalled being at Blackpool as a boy, walking towards the seafront, the wind so strong you could literally lean into it and not fall over. But one poor man had his suitcase snatched by the wind, the fastenings came undone and all his clothes blew all over the road.

I constantly marvel at the many kinds of love I have experienced and continue to experience. From that of

Ethel Spencer-Pickering, about whom I wrote in my memoirs. Although there was some fifty years between us, the love went deep, and so it continues, even in my nineties. The secret is in learning to accept the many varieties of love. Also knowing that one is never alone, for as Dr Eben Alexander writes, 'We have other family, beings who are watching and looking out for us, beings who are waiting to help us navigate our time here on earth. None of us is ever unloved.'

## 5 JANUARY

Thinking about my friendship with the lodger and his email just now – he's just arrived for a week's holiday in the Canary Islands. I write, 'How I bless your presence in my life, so totally unlooked for, so unexpected, and yet some synchronicity seems to have been at work in bringing us together.'

There is a gap of 52 years between us and yet clearly there is a deep bonding, though it has nothing to do with sex or being 'in love'. I simply know that I am there for him, and he responds in his own way, but always truthfully.

## 6 JANUARY

My friend and contemporary at Oxford, Keith Anderson, has been reminding me of those early years. I had visited Ampleforth Abbey early in 1949 and asked the Abbot if I might join the community. He sagely suggested I should go to St Benet's Hall, the Benedictine house of studies in Oxford, to take a degree 'and find out more what kind of person you are and what kind of people monks are.' Keith was supposed to have joined the community at Ampleforth but decided instead to read Greats at Wadham, but he used to attend the weekly tea party at St Benet's, which is how we first met.

There were also regular tea parties at the Catholic Chaplaincy hosted by Monsignor Val Elwes. Upstairs was a long hall used by the Newman Society. I suggested to Father Val that if a stage were built at one end there could be entertainments that could raise funds for the Newman Society. He accepted my idea and so I set about raising money to build a stage and simple proscenium arch. The major fundraising event was a piano recital in the Oxford Town Hall by the distinguished pianist Kathleen Long, who kindly didn't charge. It helped that she was a Catholic. Every seat was sold and afterwards, over a meal, she asked how I had managed to do this, telling me of an experience she had had during the war when she had been invited to perform for a charity in Leamington Spa. 'I said yes, but on condition that the recital was well advertised, that someone would meet me off the train, and that there would be a heated dressing room. Well, when I arrived there was no one to meet me, and I looked in vain for posters until eventually I found one in a butcher's shop, and made my way to the venue, where I found a small group of people waiting for the building to be opened. The dressing room was frigid and I played to a tiny audience. So, how did you manage to pack the Oxford Town Hall?'

I then told her how for several Sundays I had groups of fellow students standing outside the main Catholic Church in Oxford, as well as the Chaplaincy, selling tickets in aid of the Newman Society. And when the Candlelight Theatre – as it was called – was built, the first person to perform on its stage was the then unknown Maggie Smith.

Keith also describes attending Mass at Blackfriars, as I did regularly, when Father Gervase Mathews was celebrating. 'One never knew,' says Keith, 'what was Dominican rite and what might be a lapse of memory.' Father Gervase was a brilliant scholar, and quite an eccentric, but his homilies were mesmerising. Standing on the chancel steps, swaying slightly, he would talk quietly, almost to himself, sharing deep insights. I also recall sitting next to him in the Refectory one day for lunch – I had by then become a Dominican Tertiary – and while we were all waiting in silence to be served, he took up the bottle of tomato sauce, unscrewed the top, and solemnly poured it onto his plate in the form of a cross. Having done this, he put the screw back on the bottle, and sliding his hands inside the sleeves of his habit, sat contemplating the tomato sauce cross!

Tomorrow, being the first Sunday in the month, our meditation group meets here. Although I have meditated for over 50 years, and written two books on the subject (*Inner Journey: Outer Journey, and Finding Silence*), and though I once led a weekend meditation retreat for some 300 Catholics in Dun Laoghaire, I am not an authority on the subject nor am I a teacher of meditation. And so I would never have dreamed of setting up a meditation group. But this is what happened some twelve years ago. In 2006 The London Centre for Psychotherapy had a year of lectures under the title Psychoanalysis and Spirituality, and I was invited to give one of the talks under the title, 'What is Spirituality?' It was as a result of this paper that Celia Read, the chair of the Centre, asked if I would host a monthly meditation group in my flat.

## 8 JANUARY

Today I spend three hours at University College Hospital having two x-rays; one was an MRI, lasting 35 minutes in a tube, excruciatingly painful on my right ear. I survived by concentrating on the first five decades of the Rosary. It is the second decade that intrigues me, not just the generosity of Mary, herself pregnant, making the journey to stay with her cousin Elizabeth who, late in life, is unexpectedly pregnant, but the reaction of the child in Elizabeth's womb as though recognising the child in Mary's womb. These two boys grew up knowing each other and as teenagers onwards must have shared many conversations. John must surely have influenced Jesus with many of his ideas, while also recognising the special qualities in Jesus as the expected teacher. Yet I am not aware of anyone having written about this.

## 9 JANUARY

The scan revealed that the infection has spread to the bone and so I have to go in to UCH for a few days to receive intravenous antibiotics, and am waiting to hear – I have packed a bag in readiness, but imagine finding a spare bed at this time of the year will take time. So, the readiness is all.

Have just had a phone call. I don't have to go in to UCH today. The specialist, plus the radiologist, will look at my scans tomorrow and then decide whether or not I need to go into hospital. Anyway, my bag is packed, but I rather hope I may not have to go.

I am not letting the lodger know anything about this.

## 10 JANUARY

This laptop is often quite wayward. For instance, every time I type my surname it comes up as Rose Evans... And I am reminded of how when, many years ago, I wrote c/o The *Observer*, to the painter David Inshaw about his famous painting, now in the Tate, of two girls playing badminton in front of a very high yew hedge. He wrote back saying, 'Dear Jane Rose Evans, if ever you are in Bristol, I would love to meet.' I had to disillusion him but we became good friends. On another occasion I was publicly introduced as James Booze Evans, and once I was addressed as James Loose Evans! Ah, well, what's in a name?

This afternoon I did some shopping, and walking back I was very conscious of Hywel walking beside me. Nothing was said but I felt a comforting presence at this time of acute pain. How is one to explain this? It does not seem to me a figment of my imagination.

Tomorrow morning I have to be at the ENT hospital in Gray's Inn Road and to take what I may need in case they decide to send me on to UCH for antibiotics inserted intravenously over a few days. The lodger has sent a lovely message from the Canary Islands where he feels rejuvenated. He knows nothing of what has been going on.

11 JANUARY

Dutifully I take a cab and report to the ENT hospital in Grays Inn Road, where they seem to have no knowledge of my appointment, so I take a cab to University College Hospital where nothing seems to be known.

But after half an hour I am taken to Emergency. Another long long wait and then I am told they are expecting me at Gray's Inn Road and apologise for the mistake, so back I go in another cab. There my ear is first cleaned out, and a polyp is discovered which was then cauterised. I am told to return on Monday morning and that if there is no improvement then I will have to go into hospital for three weeks (!) for intravenous antibiotics.

## 12 January

I sleep heavily till 10 30, and then go shopping. The lodger emails that he has boarded the plane and will be back by 10 pm.

Once when Celia was staying in Wales with Hywel and myself, she asked why, when he and I had our civil partnership ratified in County Hall, Llandrindod Wells, we had not had some form of ceremony, especially as I have done so much to help others create rituals for various occasions. I replied that it was because Hywel and I had, at the stage, been committed to one another for forty-seven years at a very deep level. We had come through various crises and grown strong. What would a formal exchange of vows mean since we had already lived those vows without taking them! It was this deep sense of commitment, of discipline and selflessness that so many fail to understand. They see only lust and not love.

I keep coming across entries in old notebooks of things I have written. And now here is one that does surprise me, though in the third person clearly I am writing about myself. 'At the moment of his death the house was full of music, Bach's 'Wachet Auf', filling every room and, above all, the room in which he lay with a smile upon his face. He had once said that if at the moment of his death he heard the music of Bach he would know that all was well. He had come home.'

Just as I was writing this the lodger returns from his week's break in the Canary Islands. He is stunned to hear about my scan and possibly having to go into hospital for three weeks.

He says, 'Answer me truthfully, are you frightened?' and I reply, 'No. It is not life threatening, but even if it were I am ready to die when the time comes. I have lived my life to the full, and just as I had no fears when Hywel was dying, nor have I for myself.' I then read him the words I had found about the Bach.

Curiously, the lodger also loves 'Watchet Auf', and often sings the main chorus.

In another notebook I come across quotes I have written down from *The Face Before I Was Born* by Llewellyn Vaughan-Lee, the Sufi master. Here is one: 'From heart to heart love's potency is passed. The greatness of the path always amazes me, how people are at the right place at the right time when their heart needs to know its connection... I have come to sense the underlying web that holds us together.' And I think this was true of my meeting Hywel, and in the same, totally unexpected way, of how the lodger has come into my life.

## 13 JANUARY

Dan has had two falls down a staircase over the past few years. I recall Hywel saying to me as I used to hurtle down the 72 stairs from our attic flat at Belsize Park Gardens, 'Hold on to the bannister!' and that brought back a memory of when I was directing the legendary Edwige Feuillère in Paris in the French production of Hugh Whitemore's play *The Best of Friends*, which I had directed in London with Rosemary Harris, Sir John Gielgud and Ray McAnally. During rehearsals one day Edwige had such pain in her neck that one of her fellow actors suggested she lie down. Then in her eighties, she replied with passion, 'Non! Si je cesse maintenant, je cesse toujours!' and on we went with the rehearsal. Later she told me that the pain was the result of having been in the stage production of *The Eagle has Two Heads* in Paris with Jean Marais. At one point she had to fall down a staircase and land with her neck on a particular step. 'I am now paying the price for that!'

I have another memory of when she played the famous Abbess of Stanbrook Abbey, Dame Laurentia McLachlan, in Worcester. At one point in rehearsal I had to say to her, 'Dear Edwige, you are being much too flirtatious for an enclosed nun!' to which she replied with a grin, 'Darling James, you forget I have the reputation of being the great courtesan of the French cinema!' and then went on stage, and reined in her performance.

Like all great actors, Gielgud included, she had a deep humility and kept saying, 'You will give me notes won't you?'

And likewise, though I am in my 90th year, I am grateful to younger friends who are prepared to be truthful, and admonish me occasionally. It is all too easy for the elderly to become set in their ways, and to resist change.

## 14 January

Bronwen Astor has just died, who was a patron of the Bleddfa Trust and a good friend. It was she who alerted me to a book by Elleke van Kraalingen, a Dutch psychologist, who in the spring of 1999, when she was thirty one years old, was on holiday in Jamaica with her partner, Hermod, a 45-year-old Norwegian doctor. They were returning home to Holland, looking forward to being married, and on their last evening decided to take a late night swim. As they crossed the road a speeding car knocked Hermod down and killed him instantly. After his death he 'appeared' to her frequently, as she describes in her book, *Love Beyond Death*, saying to her, 'I am still here. And our relationship does continue. There is no death, there is no time, there is only reality. Our relationship continues in another reality, in timelessness.'

Towards the end of her book Elleka adds 'I see that we can let go of each other in the course of time and we will each grow further. His life is continuing in realms beyond my reach, and lives where he has other relationships. And I see that in timelessness we are connected as souls. I see that we are part of a group of souls in a realm where personal does not apply any more; where strengths are combined in service of a purpose beyond personal fulfilment. I feel trust in life, in the laws of the universe. I trust that we shall each grow according to our fullest potential.'

This last sentence is also my own prayer. I continue to love Hywel deeply and to feel his presence close. I know I am not alone for he is closer than close, and yet I do not cling to him. Already in this life, while depending on one another in many ways, we had also learned how to be physically apart from one another yet always knowing we were deeply bonded. I know that we were entrusted to one another from our first meeting, each learning from the other, each growing, and now we travel on. None of us owns anything or anyone.

As Elleka says, whatever existence awaits us after death will be very different to the one we know, though

I am confident that I shall 'know' Hywel again, but I am also aware that, even in this existence, we possess no one. We are each entrusted to one another for a certain period. I believe that in the next stage we shall each have tasks to perform. We live not for ourselves but for others.

It is interesting that Jung had a near-death experience when he had a heart attack in 1944. It was not, he wrote, a product of the imagination – the visions and the experiences were utterly real; there was nothing subjective about them – they all had a quality of absolute objectivity. 'On empirical grounds,' he wrote, 'I am convinced that the soul is a part outside space and time. Similarly the continuation of personal consciousness after death appears to me, on grounds of experience, to be probable.'

Increasingly I believe that there is a profound creative intelligence underlying the universe, that everything in the cosmos is interconnected, as Eastern philosophy has taught for centuries. We are not alone.

15 JANUARY

This morning at the ENT Hospital in Gray's Inn Road, the specialist said that as the ear infection has spread to the bone 'we have to take this seriously', and so either tomorrow or on Wednesday I am to go in to University College Hospital for two weeks of intravenous antibiotics. The polyp that was cauterised on Thursday has grown again so that will have to be removed. The lodger is being wonderfully supportive and will liaise with Celia, Norman, Anne and Chris, regarding visits (no one else), and he will also bring hot food in a flask for me, as hospital food is so inadequate. Meanwhile Anne says that, as a result of the antibiotics, I will need plenty of rice, lentils and yoghurt. I am so aware that I do not entertain angels unaware. And give thanks for friendship and love.

I have a strong sense that the lodger is more stunned by my news than I.

I realise that today, when the specialist said 'we have to take this seriously', at my age it might suggest my end is nearer than I thought. I don't think it is yet! But one must be prepared to let go and move on when the time does come! To set sail on the next voyage.


17 January


The lodger accompanies me to UCH, insisting on carrying the heaviest bags. He stays about two hours and in due course, after antibiotic injections, I am now in the Acute Assessment Unit on the first floor. It is possible I might only be here for six days rather than two weeks, it depends on the impact of the antibiotics. My aim is to use this time as a form of retreat… it reminds me of that wonderful line of Paulina in *The Winter's Tale*, 'this action that I go on is for my better grace.'

6 p.m. and the lodger has just been in, a great lift of the spirits to see him, and a warm hug. He came bearing the most delicious chicken casserole in a thermos flask, and yet more yoghurt.

## 18 JANUARY

A sleepless night, freezing with only one blanket, while during the night two patients are wheeled away in their beds at 1 30 a.m. to be replaced by two new patients arriving at 2 a.m. The next morning the doctor in charge of infectious diseases comes to visit me, and says I am to go home and take a course of antibiotics and see her Monday week. If they don't do the trick then I will have to go in to hospital. The lodger and Chris visited at 3 30 and again at 8 30 to help pack my bags, hail a cab, and home! Chris brings me a large bottle of Islay whisky, which has this wonderful taste of peat. Back home I am given marvellous chicken broth and then to bed.

## 19 JANUARY

I sleep till midday. The lodger is halfway through his preparing a kedgeree when he discovers that the smoked haddock I had bought and put in the fridge is nowhere to be found. I say that perhaps Sharon, who was here this morning to clean and also clean out the fridge, might have thrown it away, thinking it was of no use. The lodger says 'No, don't ring Sharon', but I do and leave a message. Eventually the lodger finds the fish, unopened, thrown in the dustbin outside! And so he is able to make the dish. Sharon rings and says she threw it away thinking it past its sell-by date! What domestic dramas. I shall shortly, at 8 p.m., retire to bed, so as not to overdo things. Anne came and gave me an excellent Alexander lesson, then drove me to M&S at South End Green so I could stock up with food and not rely on the lodger to go on feeding me.

## 20 January

The lodger has explained to me that I must take my antibiotics with a twelve hour gap between the two doses, and so I tapped my head before going to sleep so that I could wake up at 9 o'clock this morning, and then this evening, at the same time, take the second dose.

A few months ago I made the decision not to accept, with rare exceptions, invitations to lunch or dinner. The noise level, the high degree of egos, struggling to listen and respond, saps my energy. All this is a natural part of ageing. As Jung's colleague, Dr Marie Louise von Franz, observed: 'In old age, one turns away from outer activity more, and one begins to reflect and summarise whatever one has done up to now and what for and has it any meaning or was it meaningless.' One begins to be less concerned with details and more with overall questions: what is the meaning of life, why have I lived, was it worthwhile?

## 21 JANUARY

Sunday and it is snowing. Thick flakes as though up above they are plucking geese, the feathers falling to earth. But it is now turning to sleet as though the heavens were weeping, which with the state of the world they might well be doing.

In the night I became aware that for the first time in almost eight weeks there is no painful throbbing in my ear and no pulse beating in my skull, so clearly the antibiotics are beginning to work.

## 22 JANUARY

I am sipping a glass of the Islay whisky, which Chris bought for me in hospital last Thursday.

## 23 JANUARY

Reflection: There is within each one of us all the wisdom that we shall ever need, as that remarkable young woman, Etty Hillesum, who died at Auschwitz, learned. 'Listening to what is going on inside you,' she wrote, 'you acquire a kind of calm that illumines the whole day. I listen all day to what is inside me, even when I am with others, I am able to draw strength from the most deeply hidden source within myself.'

24 JANUARY

Thinking about the source of intimations and dreams, I am reminded of what Rupert Sheldrake and Mathew Fox say in their book *The Physics of Angels*, that the universe is much vaster and more amazing and constantly expanding than we had ever imagined. We are also picking up light from billions of years ago. There are also a billion galaxies in the heavens and, they suggest, there may be a governing intelligence for each galaxy.

25 JANUARY

When I left hospital I was prescribed a dose of Ciprofloxacin, two tablets of 500 grams and two of 250 grams. Because I did not read the instructions carefully – typical of my impatience, I have been taking a double dose every day. Now for the final week I shall just take the proper dose, but this may explain why I have felt weak and woozy – when will I learn! Also not to drink red wine which brings on gout! Pull yourself together, James!

## 26 January

Very much below par today and inclined to be tetchy. This intense cold weather doesn't help either. Difficult to order one's thoughts. Yet the rose tree in its plastic pot, waiting to be planted, is already sprouting green leaves so maybe I am also. I manage to do some more work on the last draft of *A Life Shared*, about my life with Hywel.

The response to my new book *Blue Remembered Hills – A Radnorshire Journey* has taken me by surprise.

The ache in the ear and jaw seems constant now, though I am able to sleep. However, on Monday, I am at the ENT Hospital in Gray's Inn Road and told I may have to be there for two to three hours, so my hope is they will remove the polyp that has grown inside the ear which, I suspect, is now the main cause. What a long haul it has been – two whole months!

## 27 January

It is true I am a Christian, albeit much influenced by Buddhist and Sufi writings. However, although ordained, I am less and less a Church man. I do not mean to say the Church and churches are valueless, any more than are synagogues and temples, but I have moved beyond. I cannot believe that Jesus is God, the Second Person of the Trinity. Rather he is the most remarkable of all spiritual teachers, whose message was simple: Love God with all your heart, and Love your neighbour as yourself. In addition, he was psychologically accurate when he said, 'The Kingdom of Heaven is within.'

On 6 December 1273 in Naples, Thomas Aquinas, the greatest theologian the Church has known, while celebrating Mass that morning had a vision, the details of which he never revealed. But from that day, Aquinas, the author of more than 40 books, never wrote another word, but devoted himself to prayer till the day of his death. Until then he had been engaged on his greatest work, *The Summa Theologica*, but when his spiritual director urged him to complete it, he replied 'After what I have seen, all that I have written seems like straw.'

Why did this prodigious scholar, not yet 50, so abruptly abandon the crowning achievement of his life's work? Three months later he was dead. What, clearly, Aquinas came to perceive is that the essence of things is beyond the reach of the rational mind. As Hamlet says, 'The rest is silence'. And yet out of what Aquinas wrote in the unfinished *Summa* the Church, ignoring his final statement, fashioned the catechism, reducing what he had written to a book of rules and regulations, burying the simple teachings of Jesus under a vast basilica of theology. The lesson of ulti-mate silence has yet to be learned by the Churches; only the Society of Friends offers worship in silence. A small boy once said to me with some passion, 'God is a feel, not a think!' He was right. In spite of all the books of theology, belief in a God is purely intuitive, subjective and why some believe and some do not remains a mystery.

As Reza Aslan says in his book *God*, 'God is pure existence, without name, essence or personality.' St Paul comes closest to this in his wonderful phrase in which he likens God to 'that in which we live and move and have our being'. The idea of a personalised God is a projection on our part. God is not a person, but the ocean in which we swim.

## 28 JANUARY

Sunday and I shopped early as Norman is coming to supper this evening. I make a Waldorf salad, and prepare chicken breasts with a mixture of cream cheese and basil pesto, covered with a slice of parma ham and sage leaves.

## 29 JANUARY

Off to the ENT Hospital in Gray's Inn Road where the specialist informs me that the polyp has gone. He then had a long telephone conversation with Dr Logan at the Hospital for Tropical Diseases whom I see next Monday, and she said she wanted me to continue with the antibiotics for a further four weeks. Roman, the doctor I was seeing today, will also arrange a fresh scan. Having gone to the hospital in a cab I economised by coming back on the 46 bus.

## 30 JANUARY

In the night, I found myself reflecting on how ordinary lives can be made extraordinary by simple acts of generosity, of kindness. So that over time they add up to a kind of rosary of goodness, one bead, one action, after the other. One doesn't have to subscribe even to any religious practice. Young Etty Hillesum who, at the age of 28, was to go to Auschwitz of her own choice to be with and support her family, had no religious background, never went near a synagogue or a rabbi but on her own initiative began to meditate. As Patrick Woodhouse observes in his book, *A Life Transformed*, 'She was not a religious person, at least not in the institutional sense of that word. This makes her a woman for our time, when institutional spirituality is in decline and yet the hunger for authentic spirituality is more keenly felt than ever. Etty speaks across the boundaries of religions.'

## 31 JANUARY

Travelling in a cab to the audiologist in Wigmore Street I saw a white van with the name 'Chapel and Swan' on the side, and thought how if Mr Swan had been named Church, then it would have read 'Chapel and Church'.

The lodger plays for me Gorecki's 'Third Symphony', which I have not heard for twenty years or more. I remember first hearing it on the radio. I was alone and began to move with the music and it led to my leading a workshop called 'Journey to the Mother', which was very, very powerful. The first movement contains a lament for a female voice, that of Mary standing at the foot of the cross.

# FEBRUARY 2018

## 1 FEBRUARY

Vaughan wrote, 'Prayer is the world in tune' and this reminds me of some words of Fr Henri Le Saux, or as he preferred to be known, Abhishkinanda, 'The important thing is to fix the mind on something that leads to transcendence and frees from wandering thoughts.' If thoughts still come they should be like birds flying in the open space of the heart, over my head, without disturbing me.'

## 2 FEBRUARY

One of the most haunting sentences in the Gospels is that spoken by Jesus in the garden at Gethsemane, knowing he was about to be arrested and sentenced to death.

Knowing what lay ahead, Jesus sweats with terror, and needs the comfort of his three closest friends, but they, exhausted by the emotion of the last meal they had all shared, were asleep. 'Could you not watch with me one hour?' says Jesus. It was reflecting on those words that I began about two years ago to keep watch with those who were about to have an operation, or go up for a crucial interview. I am not praying but simply keeping watch. I am not to know whether it has any effect on the other person, though it does help if one is facing an operation or a crucial interview to know that someone is there, quietly supporting. It may also have a telepathic effect, something is transmitted. Who knows? All I can do is be obedient to this instinct to support others in this way.

I have been pondering some words spoken by the late Archbishop of Milan, Cardinal Maria Martini, in a death bed interview: 'Our culture has aged, our churches are big and empty, and the church bureaucracy rises up – our rituals and our cassocks are pompous. The Church must admit its mistakes and begin a radical change, starting from the Pope and the bishops.' This, of course, is what Pope Francis is trying to set in motion but he is up against a deep opposition.

Similarly in the 1980s the late Father Pedro Arrupe, the influential Superior General of the Jesuit order, observed, 'I am afraid that we are about to offer yesterday's answers to tomorrow's problems, that we are talking in such a way that people no longer understand us, that we are using a language that doesn't go to the hearts of men and women. If that is the case, then we'll talk a great deal but only to ourselves. In fact, no one will be listening to us anymore, because no one will grasp what we are trying to say.' Even more surprising were the words of that prince among Popes, Pope Pius X11, to a gathering of cardinals shortly before his death, as reported at the time in *The Tablet*, 'The Roman Church must not seek to embrace the entire world. It must learn to accept that there are other faiths, other creeds, and other temperaments.' He also, when sending Vatican delegates to Libya said, 'Do not think that you are going among infidels. Muslims also have salvation – the ways of Providence are infinite.'

For myself I cannot believe in the division of faiths. There can be but one God, whether called Allah or Ram, and there can be but one family of God. The truth shines with its own light, and often in unexpected places. Each of us approaches the Eternal along a particular path: cultural, geographical, biographical. As Dom Bede Griffiths said, 'I do not feel that religions can simply go on following their own paths separately. We have reached a point in evolution where we have to meet. We have to share, to discover one another.' Yet again I am reminded of some words spoken by one of the characters in Christopher Fry's, *A Sleep of Prisoners*:

Affairs are now soul-size.
The enterprise is exploration into God, Where are
you making for? It takes
So many thousand years to wake,
But will you wake, for pity's sake?

4 FEBRUARY, SUNDAY

Today I was suddenly reminded of an incident in New
York in 1956 when I was teaching at the Julliard School
of music. One of the students asked if he could come
and talk to me. Aged 24, he was a professional skater,
who had played the juvenile lead in *Chase* and had been
invited by Tom Arnold to skate in London but decided
he should study dance at the Juilliard. We talked until
two in the morning by which time I was lying sleep-
ily on the floor. Suddenly he said, 'Put your hands up
in the air, bend your elbows and open your legs.' He
then placed both his hands on mine and did a hand-
stand, his legs up in the air, his face looking down into
mine. He seemed to be floating above me, diving down
towards me, like an image from a painting by Chagall.
'Come down – I want to kiss you!' I said. He laughed
and descended. We didn't kiss, and shortly after he left,
but it remains for me one of the most erotic moments
in my life.

5 FEBRUARY

A new rota at the meditation group began yesterday when Tusse gave the talk, and Anne will speak in April, and I every other month. In this way, I am able to step back, and allow individual members to share with us something of their own richness. It is such a strong group that this is important.

Today it is so cold that my brain freezes up and I have nothing to record except that at 3.30 a cab comes to take me to Dr Logan at the Hospital for Tropical Diseases to see how my ear infection is progressing. The antibiotics make me slightly dizzy and tired.

It seems that in the old days you could die of the kind of infection I have had. She has now extended my antibiotics for a further two weeks, six in all.

Watched a film on my computer about Stanley Spencer's two elderly daughters, characters straight out of Beckett!

6 FEBRUARY

I get up to turn on a hot bath when I am drenched by cold water from the shower. The lodger has been using cold water. I turn the wrong tap in panic and in seconds the floor, door and passage outside are covered with water. Because I never use the shower I don't know how to turn it off and in the process get even more drenched. In the end I find the right taps. The shock at first startles me fully awake and then I laugh at the comedy of it all. The lodger is full of apologies, but I think it is splendid for someone of my age to have such a shock. It amused me. May I never become staid – though I think that most unlikely.

7 FEBRUARY

What happened? I have no memory of the day. I suspect it is the extreme cold freezing up the brain and memory, but it was an early night because of having to leave here the next day to do a broadcast with Mark Tully for his programme *Something Understood*.

8 FEBRUARY

I arrive at the studios but there are technical hitches due to the reception from Delhi where Mark Tully is in a studio with an Indian engineer. Eventually they have to move to another studio and after half an hour we begin. In one of his questions relating to the famous Joseph Campbell dictum 'Follow your bliss', I explain that bliss does not mean selfishly going one's own way and to hell with everyone else. Although Jesus was a carpenter, at the age of thirty he realised his life was to be very different. And when he went into the desert for forty days, we read how 'He was alone with the wild

beasts and angels came and comforted him.' Obviously
there would be wild beasts in the desert but it is also an
image of his own inner demons that he had to confront,
what in Jungian terms would be called his 'shadow' side.
It was then that he realised that if he were to spread the
message that he felt compelled to do, to 'follow his bliss'
– this would eventually lead to arrest and an appalling
death by crucifixion. Yet Jesus followed his bliss and so
at the end was able to say, 'Father, I have done the work
that you sent me to do'. May that be said by all of us.

9 FEBRUARY

Even colder today, but twice went to the shops, and then
returned to work on my talk for our meditation group in
March, as well as type out some extracts from an article
by Brother Wayne Teadale OSB on monastic life, extracts
which are equally relevant to couples living together. The
monastic life, he says, teaches one an attitude of acceptance of others, non-judgement and compassion. 'It is
particularly the community that slowly wears and tears
away the ego, the defences, and the excuses built up over
years. While others may annoy us, they also provide
opportunities for growth by challenging us to understand
and love others.' If only couples would learn this.

I have been reflecting how there have been in my life
certain projects that I have failed to achieve. One was
an adaptation I wrote of the psalms, for a company of

forty non-professional actors, their ages ranging from nine to ninety. The psalms were broken up into sections, some to be spoken by individuals, some by the whole company. The idea was to present this in a country church, starting at midnight and ending at dawn with the actors and audience all enjoying a simple breakfast.

The psalms express the yearnings of a whole nation over centuries as they sought a promised land. But there is a deeper meaning to this image, beyond the territorial, one that Herman Hesse examines in his novella, *Journey to the East*. In it he says, 'I realised that I had joined a pilgrimage to the East, seemingly a definite and single pilgrimage – but in reality, in its broadest sense, this expedition to the East was not only mine and now; this procession of believers and disciples had always and incessantly been moving towards the East, towards the House of Light and each member, each group, indeed our whole host and its great pilgrimage, was only a wave in the eternal stream of human beings towards the East, towards Home. The knowledge passed through my mind like a ray of light and immediately reminded me of a phrase by the poet Novalis, 'Where are we really going? Always home!'

## 10 FEBRUARY

An email arrives from my friend Diana, who is a Quaker and a prison visitor. She writes, 'I took your book on meditation, *Finding Silence*, into the prison with me the other day and talked about 'bluebottle thoughts' as you describe them, with a very angry young man who is finding it hard to find any peace. It was a good piece to use as a starting point and notice-ably in the conversation that followed to observe his anger level decreasing.

Not an easy conversation as he was in his cell and I was outside speaking to him through a letter-box style hatch in his door – not the easiest way to find some quiet, but needs must.'

It is a heart-aching story and she has many such to tell. The conditions under which the prisoners live – there is so much work to be done and so much prayer needed.

## 11 FEBRUARY

Amy to lunch and I tried the leg of lamb with paste made of preserved lemons, rosemary, garlic and salt, but in the end prefer my old method of covering it with flour then inserting sprigs of rosemary – also I don't like pink meat. Norman comes to supper and we have cold lamb and end with a wonderful fruity Christmas pudding from M&S. His house has been invaded by mice that have eaten through the electric wires, and so there is no heating and all the food in the freezer had to be thrown away. An electrician came several times and the last time spent six hours trying to track where mice enter. Although Norman put down mousetraps, the mice have learned how to extricate the cheese without being caught. Is there now a new race of Super Mice?! On top of all this a fox spilled the contents of a bag of rubbish all over the garden.

12 FEBRUARY

Two hours wait at the ENT Hospital, so I meditated for one and half of those hours. Then I saw the specialist who reported the ear is now clean as a whistle. It is freezing cold and snow is predicted.

7 30 p.m. and I shall retire early to bed, curl up in my nest. It is too cold, even with the heating on, and too dark. But, come the spring – and already green blades of narcissi and daffodils are springing up sturdily in my urns, and the roses sprouting tiny green leaves. The great lesson of nature is that when everything seems dead or dormant, new life is beginning.

Dominique, who gardens for me, emails me to say how her daughter is in Calais cooking and feeding the hundreds of young and old refugees who have nowhere to go and nothing to eat. 'I am so proud of her!' she adds. It baffles me that our affluent society is unable to tackle this problem. Even in this country surely it is possible for churches, synagogues and mosques to unite in welcoming the stranger in our midst. That would be a start. Most churches today in cities have toilet and kitchen facilities, and so could accommodate many over-night. I think of what the great St Vincent de Paul and Abbé Pierre achieved in France, Elizabeth Fry in England, Dorothy Day in America, and most strikingly of all, against all odds, Mother Teresa of Calcutta.

## 13 FEBRUARY

Go for my warfarin test, which is now back to a normal reading. A cold wet walk back.

## 14 FEBRUARY

Walking back, dragging behind me a heavy load of shopping, it is so cold that an inch and a half of snot hangs from my nose and I think any moment it will turn into an icicle for it is freezing. However, I stop to blow my nose and am now back in the warmth of the flat.

## 15 FEBRUARY

I retire to my bed just after 8 p.m. Like many elderly people I find the long dark tunnel of winter depressing and so escape to the warmth of my burrow. But there is more to it than that. While I have dealt well with the loss of Hywel, nonetheless I miss his physical presence intensely, his just being there. With the death of one's

partner one is thrown back on one's self, and the awareness that half of one's self is missing, like losing a limb.

At half past eleven I woke and thought how deeply I
long to be hugged and held in a warm embrace, not for
any sexual reasons – I am long past all that, but for the
deep comfort of being held. And I realise how many
old people must yearn to be held, embraced – indeed,
some may never have known it. Which is why, as Keith
Hunt at the Royal Free, whose team give massages to
over 35,000 people a year, says that for many old people
it is the first time of being caressed for many a long year.

## 16 FEBRUARY

It is just after one o'clock in the morning and I am
again awake. Whenever I wake in the night I mentally
repeat my mantra.

And I know that I am held in a deeper embrace than
that of any human being, that I am upheld, as we all
are, by a deep Love 'in which we live and move and
have our being.' The human embrace is simply a brief
glimpse of the eternal embrace.

## 17 FEBRUARY

Anne comes to give me my weekly Alexander lesson.
I finish reading Bennet's book of meetings with Jung,
and have left it out for the lodger to read. I then retire

to bed even earlier this evening, at 7 p.m., but now at 9.30 a.m. have woken and realise I have to deal with this retreat which is more than winter darkness or the effect of the antibiotics. I have to acknowledge that what is hitting me hard, five years and more after Hywel's death, is his physical absence and all that our shared life meant to each and both of us. For the first three and a half years I seemed to be dealing with his loss in a very positive way, helped by a frequent awareness of his presence, and the conviction that he was helping me, but now it is as though he is moving on to other responsibilities. He will always be there for me, as I for him, but I am aware that in that other existence, of which I have no doubt, each will have new tasks, new responsibilities on a continuing journey of discovery. In writing the book *A Life Shared*, I was able to canalise much of my pain and sense of loss. That is now done and I am faced with an inner emptiness. I miss the hours we would be together, he in his chair reading, I at my desk working, and occasionally one of us would look up and catch the other's eye and smile. Now I sit alone in this handsome large room lined with books, except on those few occasions when the lodger may drop in to chat or, more rarely, but blessedly, will lie on the sofa, reading and listening to music.

I begin to understand what mothers experience when their children grow up and leave home or die unexpectedly.

And this brings back memories of my own mother, both her courage in breaking away from my father and living on her own, but missing me, and this became especially marked in old age.

I was her emotional anchor and always after visiting her at the Old Rectory at Bleddfa she would feel the loneliness so intensely that she would open every door, so as not to feel shut in. And whenever I left she would embrace me tightly, her cornflower blue eyes brimming with tears. I was all she had.

I think of the many thousands of women who, as a result of the First World War, and other wars, lost their sons and husbands, and had to live only with a memory. Death is brutal, as Jung said, when his wife Emma died.

I know that I have to draw on all that I have learned from years of analysis, and from all the interior work I have done, also by reaching out to others: those who come with deep needs and questions. And so tomorrow I need to make the effort not to retreat to bed so early but endure the darkness and the emptiness. I am blessed that I can write, but otherwise much of my physical appetite for food, and for other activities, reading, watching television, listening to music, I neglect. That is not good. Television I can do without but I must get back into the habit of listening to music, and more persistent reading. It is all a matter of discipline. At least I don't lean unduly on my friends, though inevitably the lodger, being at close quarters and so observant, will have been aware of the undercurrents. But one is comforted by small acts of friendship, as when Johanna calls with a tub of apple or apricot compote, or Pat with a broth of chicken and rice, or the lodger leaving small delicious offerings of food on my desk, or Celia accompanying me to the Hospital for Tropical Diseases. One is never ultimately alone.

18 FEBRUARY, SUNDAY

I am rereading for the umpteenth time Eliot's *The Four Quartets* and the phrase that leaps out at me today is:

'The only wisdom we can hope to acquire
  Is the wisdom of humility. Humility is endless.'

Marvellous!

The lodger has just served a splendid lunch of poached cod with couscous and a sauce, followed by an Ivy dessert: frozen berries with hot melted white chocolate!

I have been out sweeping up leaves from the patio, encouraged by a burst of sun and the sight of sturdy spears of green from narcissi, daffodils and tulips, springing up in my tubs. When the weather is warmer I must invite the members of our meditation group to gather in a circle in the garden and sense all nature around us.

19 FEBRUARY

Following on from above it seems increasingly clear to me that all our lives are inseparably involved with one another. No one lives alone. As the character played by James Dean, in the film *Rebel Without a Cause*, cries out at one point, 'But Mam, we are all involved!'

I go shopping in Waitrose on the Finchley Road, I had to lay in food as I have various friends coming to lunch. Harriet on Thursday, Selina next Tuesday, Stephanie on the Thursday, and Ken on the Friday. Clearly my energy is returning!

I am reading the most extraordinary book, *Wonder Beyond Belief: On Christianity* by Navid Kermani, a devout Muslim. His chapter entitled 'Humiliation', a meditation upon Caravaggio's The Crowning with Thorns, ought to be read in every church on Maundy Thursday.

20 FEBRUARY

To Amplifon to have my hearing aids adjusted, then back for a lunch of delicious onion soup with grated gruyère. And now this evening a rich chicken broth with rice! I'm rereading Jung's *Psychology and Religion* and am struck as on first reading, by one patient's dream in which he enters a solemn house which is called 'the house of inner composure or self-collection.'

Then a voice is heard saying, 'Woe to those who use religion as a substitute for the other side of life. Religion is no substitute, but it is the ultimate accomplishment added to every other activity of the soul.' And then come these amazing words: 'Out of the fullness of life thou shalt give birth to thy religion, only then shalt thou be blessed.'

Each of us comes to the Divine by different paths, but all point in the same direction.

## 21 FEBRUARY

I am rereading Patrick Woodhouse's *Etty Hillesum: A Life Transformed*. Today when so many have problems with established religion, she is an inspiration on how one can find God deep within, without going near a synagogue, church, or mosque. What became her faith was grounded in her own immediate, personal and direct experience. On her own initiative she learned to meditate, 'I listen very intently, with my whole being, and try to fathom the meaning of things.' Elsewhere she writes, 'There is a deep well inside me. And in it dwells God. Sometimes I am there too. But more often stones and grit block the well, and God is buried beneath. Then he must be dug out again.' At 29 she died in Auschwitz.

23 FEBRUARY

It is so cold that the press refers to it as 'the Beast from the East.' As I go out to the shops the lodger appears, waving a woolly hat for me to wear to cover my ears. He and Sharon this morning were discussing the rising damp in the hall and kitchen, and how best to tackle it.

24 FEBRUARY

My left foot is crippled with pain so that I hobble like an old man; it is because I started drinking red wine again. I have now stopped and am on medication that will clear it. In the evening to the Park Theatre to see a play about Princess Margaret. Not a good play and with some less than good acting in it, but Felicity Dean as the Princess is superlative. Clearly she has studied documentary films about the Princess as she not only displays her tone of voice and mannerisms, but also, like the best Stanislavski actors, has absorbed them, and become Princess Margaret! It was a riveting performance and I called out 'Bravo, Bravissimo!' at the end. It is rare to see so complete a performance.

25 FEBRUARY, SUNDAY

The wind is like an icicle.

Sorting out papers – a constant exercise – I open the

small notebook in which I record significant dreams and come across this, which I had written on Jan 20th 2017. 'My mood is such that I feel I am at the bottom of a deep well that has dried up and all I can do is wait for someone to lower a bucket and haul me up.' And then, lying awake, I recalled the drawing I did decades ago, which I describe in *Inner Journey: Outer Journey*, when I was feeling very low. I did this drawing of a Franciscan friar lowering a bucket to me at the bottom of a dried-up well... and then as I continued drawing I drew a tunnel leading off from the bottom of the well to a small cave where there was a simple stone altar and on it a single seed. I realised that it was my task to water this seed: the seed of meditation. I then did a second drawing in which the seed grew to be an enormous tree. Later, some words came to me: Go deeper and deeper, tunnel into the ground, go to earth, journey through the darkness because at the end of the tunnel there is light.'

As I have often observed to our meditation group: there is deep within us all the wisdom that we need. It is a matter always of going deeper, and not shunning the darkness.

26 February

To the hospital to see Dr Logan who says never put anything in my ears but use a few drops of oil to keep wax at bay and avoid having the ears syringed.

We are in the middle of an Arctic freeze – this morning it tried to snow, a few crumbs falling haphazardly and then ceasing. I suspect tomorrow it will either be even colder or else a deep snow, which will at least be warmer. I have been reading some short pieces by Laurie Lee in a collection called *Village Christmas*. I have never envied anyone or anything but I find myself envying his turn of phrase, that of a poet, which makes his writing glow and glisten. One can't emulate him, it is simply part of who he was and the kind of writer he was.

My printer refuses to work. I try everything possible and am in despair. The lodger comes in, on his way out, to ask me to give his best wishes to Selina who is lunching with me today. I express my despair regarding the printer and he says very sharply, 'Every time I come into this room you bark some request at me!' I apologise, explaining that I do despair at my frequent failure to understand technology, a weakness of old age. But he is right, one can become so self-centred, thinking only of one's own needs and then abruptly loading them on to someone else. So this is an important lesson for me. He finds that the problem is due to the printer needing a new cartridge, so I ring Mike Williams, knowing he had ordered three new cartridges some time back, and he will now drop them round. Today's rebuke from the lodger is rightly deserved. I realise how easy it is for the elderly to become querulous, like a spoilt child thinking only of itself.

A lovely shared time with Selina à deux, even though I had undercooked the chicken breasts! Snow fell, transforming the garden, but going out shopping later I had to walk warily, and was glad to be back in the warm.

27 February

The garden is deep in snow and more is now tumbling down at great speed, sometimes slanting to the right then changing direction according to the wind, like bags of goose-feathers being unbaled. Instead of the gentle floating of snowflakes the other day, this is a real snowstorm.

28 February

The lodger says I am not to go out and he will do what shopping I need for tomorrow when Stephanie Cole comes to lunch.

# MARCH 2019

## 1 MARCH

Steph and I have known each other for a long time and several times she came to stay with Hywel and me in Ireland. I was telling her how Molly Keane nicknamed Hywel 'Blodwyn', saying he didn't know how to lay a table, and would have to go in the morning, and she wouldn't provide a reference! Thereafter when I was cooking for guests and needed Hywel to help carry in the dishes, I would call out 'Blodwyn!' I then told Steph, who wanted to help me in the kitchen today, that Mrs Veal (my imaginary housekeeper) didn't like folk in her kitchen, and Steph recalled how once in Ireland she said to Hywel 'Shall I go and give Jimmie a hand in the kitchen?' and he replied, 'No, the Bishop wouldn't like it!'

I tell her how on one occasion when our friend Joyce Grant came to stay with Hywel and me in Cork, I suddenly rebelled at doing all the cooking and so said, 'We'll have a rota. I will cook on Mondays, Joyce on

Tuesday, Hywel Wednesdays and so on.' Monday and Tuesday went fine, but on Wednesday Hywel said with a grin, 'I think we'll eat out tonight!' So I went back to being Martha!

## 2 MARCH

The snow is even worse and much of the country is snow-bound. Sharon has arrived and with the lodger is going to tackle the damp in the hall and kitchen, then order a dehumidifier, and once dried out, arrange to have the rising damp dealt with temporarily every two or three years. The sink also is blocked, and I have had to call in Dyno-Rod three times. In the meantime I wash all dishes in the bathroom sink.

More snow is predicted for this afternoon. What moves me is the way that the green spears of tulips thrust their way upwards through the thick mats of snow on the urns.

My blog for the first of the month is out and already there have been four comments, clearly it has touched a nerve in each person. And in the light of what I wrote in this journal a few days ago about the death of Hywel now hitting me very hard, it is indeed relevant to myself!

It is entitled *Ends and Beginnings*:

'When one has been declared redundant, fired from one's job, a relationship ended, or a beloved partner dies, it is painful to let go and face the unknown. Will I ever hold down another job? How can I go on living when the one who meant most to me is no longer there?

We cannot escape this sense of desolation, nor should we attempt to do so. But each day, bit by bit, learn to confront the emptiness.

The emptiness is, of course, inside us. The work or the person that made life meaningful for us is no longer there and so we are thrown back on ourselves. We all have occasions to grieve. Think of the last lines of 'The Oven Bird' by Robert Frost:

The question that he frames in all but words
Is what to make of a diminished thing.'

We have to trust to destiny that something new does exist around the corner. As the Buddhist teacher Pema Chodron has written, 'When there's a big disappointment, we don't know if that's the end of the story. It may just be the beginning of a great adventure.' At a time of deep loss, of seeming failure, it is time to obey the command: 'Let down your nets into the deep.'

If we can go down into our own depths, face the pain and emptiness and the loneliness, we shall find new growth, new possibilities which will enable us to respond to others with a deeper understanding.'

Sharon and the lodger found that part of the reason for the blocked sink is that the U-bend tube was full of grease, so he is going also to get a new one of those. In addition they have sorted out all the linen, sheets and pillow cases, some to be discarded as they're stained with rust, some for Sharon to take to the Women's Institute along with a large bag full of balls of coloured wool. Sharon and the lodger have worked so hard all morning, with an amazing drive, and reorganised things far better than I could have done…

3 MARCH

For the past few days I have been immured, because of the deep snow and the lodger rightly saying I should not go out. Then today as the thaw began I had hoped to go to the shops, but Anne, who is here for my Alexander lesson, said it is much too slippery. All this has made me think of prisoners confined for many hours to their cells.

We still have sink trouble. I heard a sudden gurgle and it filled with dirty water. After a while it subsided only for it to well up again an hour or two later.

4 MARCH, SUNDAY

The thaw has set and the garden is once again green but the sink continues to bubble up filth and the lodger has to bale it out. We shall get a local plumber in tomorrow.

Today is our meditation group, my turn to speak.

## 5 March

Off to Amplifon to see Barry Rogers re: new hearing aids that won't block the ear, as this can cause an ear infection too. They will cost some £3,500, which I don't have, as I am about to spend £8000 plus on much needed double-glazing, but there is a scheme whereby I have a year in which to pay and so I will start to save.

I emailed the agency who manage this house on behalf of the freeholder, and they have sent a top team of plumbers to solve the problem of our sink filling up several times a day with filthy water!

## 6 March

I visit Estelle Spottiswoode, now 92, who until some months ago, in spite of cancer in the bones, heroically turned up each month for our meditation, beautifully groomed. Now she lies day after day in her bed, looked after by a wonderful carer called Margaret, as well as a back up team, all arranged privately. She stares at me but I am not sure she recognises me, she seems a long way away, and struggling with a dry throat. I sit holding her hand in total silence and then, as I rise to leave, I make the sign of the cross on her forehead. At the door Margaret, the carer, asks me to bless her also. On my return I retreat to my room to read and rest.

7 March

It was in the 1960s that I got to know Malcolm Muggeridge and his wife Kitty, often visiting them in Robertsbridge or staying with them in the south of France. Malcolm was then at the height of his popularity as a television personality and each year did a lecture tour of America. Learning that I needed to raise money for the theatre at Hampstead he arranged with his agent in New York to book me a tour. Colston Leigh was the top lecture agent then in New York and his regulars, including Malcolm, were people like Eleanor Roosevelt and others, so that I was fairly low down on the list. However, he had a handsome brochure printed about me including endorsements from Tennessee Williams, Dame Sybil Thorndike, Sir John Gielgud, Sir Michael Redgrave and others. Before I left Malcom gave me two pieces of advice: always start with a joke, and always wear good shoes. It was the latter that puzzled me. 'Because, dear boy,' he replied, 'you will be on a stage, seated at a table, and what people will see is your shoes!'

And so I set sail for the States. On arrival I met Colston Leigh, a six foot tall ex-prize boxer, who said 'I have only two pieces of advice to give you. First, it is no good just being good at this game, you have to be superlative.' To which I replied that I had every intention of being so! However his second piece of advice was more puzzling. 'The Women's Clubs at which you will be speaking on occasions will not be interested in what you have to say, only in touching.' He did not elaborate!

My first booking was at a brand new Women's Club in Houston, Texas, set among lawns, with a red carpet and liveried commissioner. Inside, the walls were hung with Impressionist paintings and Aubusson tapestries. In the dining room some 500 women sat down to a vegetarian lunch, while I was seated on a platform with the Chair-Person and other officials. Behind us was a large window with a white curtain drawn across it. As I rose to speak we all saw the silhouette of a mouse on the other side running up the curtain. At once I stood on my chair and screamed, which got my first laugh.

At the end, as I moved amongst the women, they caressed the silk scarf at my neck, touched my arm, murmuring, 'Oh, he's so purty! (pretty) so purty!' or made remarks such as 'My great grandmother came from Wales' and so on. It was then that I realised that for them I was a relic of Old England!

At one point on this first tour I came to Elon College, North Carolina, where I was to stay for a week. Dr James Elder, one of the Faculty, invited me to brunch on the Sunday to meet some of his students. When I arrived he was busily cooking bacon and eggs and wearing an apron on which was a large Union Jack. I noticed that the students were all drinking Earl Grey tea and scooping Oxford Cooper's marmalade onto their toast. In the background I could hear a recording which was the sound of cheering crowds, horses' hooves and carriage wheels. Suddenly, however, there was the burst of an organ and a vast congregation about to sing the British National Anthem. It was then that I realised we were listening to a recording of the Coronation of Queen Elizabeth the Second. And it was at this moment that the students put down their glasses and, standing to attention, solemnly sang 'God save our gracious Queen'. I was stunned. When it was over I rather shyly asked if they were doing this just for me. 'Oh, no,' they replied. 'We do this every Sunday.'

## 8 MARCH

I prepare coq-au-vin to cook tomorrow to share with the lodger.

## 9 MARCH

The lodger and Sharon tackle the dead flies behind the overhead blinds in the conservatory, it takes them an hour and a half. I go to have a massage at the Royal Free with Keith Hunt, which I have not been able to do for some months because of the ear infection but now I am back to weekly visits.

He tells me how a doctor in Hull, about to retire, heard him give a talk on YouTube about the importance of massage, especially for the elderly, and how he would like to devote his retirement to giving massages to the elderly in his area and could he come to London to learn from Keith. He came, and spent a day, and then wrote a very moving letter, enclosing a cheque for £500 for Keith's work. Keith is the only person employed by the NHS but he has launched a charity to raise money to pay his team, though quite a number of them are voluntary. Between them they now treat over 3700 patients a year. Not surprisingly, about two years ago, he was awarded an MBE for his services, but he does wonder what will happen when in eighteen months he retires after working for 50 years at the Royal Free.

## 10 MARCH

A day of domestic chores.

## 11 MARCH, SUNDAY

Rupert comes to breakfast after Mass at St. Dominic's – much rich good talk.

Chris comes to lunch – roast pork etc. He is so articulate, such good and fascinating conversations. I take a siesta, then we have tea and more talk. He leaves just after six.

## 12 March

Went to Amplifon to have new hearing aids fitted, then shopping, cooking.

## 13 March

Table laid, the coq-au-vin already cooked so will only need heating. Have prepared the vegetables; carrots, leeks, and a few mushrooms. Tusse is bringing a starter of chicory, Roquefort cheese, pear and walnuts, while Johanna is bringing an apricot pudding, and Celia bringing wine, though Piers and I will just drink the sparkling wine 'sans alcool' that I get from the Wine Society.

The evening is a great success, mainly because Piers is a splendid conversationalist, which I am not. I prefer just to listen. Hywel was the gregarious one.

## 14 March

Had hair cut by Stavros. His salon plus all adjoining buildings have been bought by a property development firm to build flats, so he has to leave by the end of the year.

Back to meet Richard Beecham who is directing the forthcoming tour of *84 Charing Cross Road* with Stefanie Powers and Clive Francis, whom I directed in *84* at Cambridge two years ago.

## 15 March

Interesting how memory has to be worked at in old age. Often I can't remember a name, or perhaps only the first name and so I then work my way through the alphabet until the name clicks into place. It is the same with doing the concise crossword each day. Often I cannot find a word but then, if I leave it for ten or so minutes, suddenly the answer comes. It means one has to work at this regularly and not become mentally lazy.

I go on the C11 bus to the Finchley Road to buy a new small coffee pot, etc. and stop off at Barretts to buy chicken breasts and legs to make two coq-au-vins, as well as a whole chicken to roast on Saturday in case the lodger would like to share it.

I find myself puzzled by the long one-sided conversations people have on their mobiles on buses, in the streets, etc. What on earth are they talking about, and why so little listening?! But then, as I have said, I am not a natural conversationalist.

## 16 March

Reading Mary Oliver's poem 'When Death Comes', I note the last line, 'I don't want to end up simply having visited this world'.

17 March, Saturday, 3 a.m.

The sense of a lessening of Hywel's presence sent me into a negative mood. But this is, I realise, an important step forward. I am learning to let go of him. So many on the death of a loved one suffer a deeply painful bereavement and weep frequently. I didn't, because I was so conscious of Hywel's presence. I never 'saw' him, as some see their departed ones, but, apart from his appearance in dreams, there were occasions when I was strongly aware of his presence, almost tangible, and I have had this sense of his keeping an eye out for me. But in the afterlife we have to allow those we love to move on. It is here that Elleke van Kraalingen's book Love Beyond Death is so rich in insights. And so for myself, knowing that all is well with Hywel, and that he is now on the next stage of his journey, it is time for me to let go, and to move on.

18 March, Sunday

The lodger plays for me today's programme, *Something Understood*, in which Mark Tully questions me about the phrase of Joseph Campbell's 'Follow your bliss', and the programme then further explores the idea through the writings of Pablo Neruda, Kathleen Raine, Stephen Spender, etc., a beautifully composed anthology of reflections.

In sorting out papers, a never-ending task, I came across a letter from John Cupper in response to my having told him of the acclaim given to Angela Lansbury in Michael Blakemore's recent production of *Blithe Spirit*, where the audience applauded every entrance and exit, and gave her a standing ovation at the end, and when Norman and I went round to see her afterwards there were some 200 people behind a barricade waiting for her to appear at the stage door. I had not experienced anything like this since Ivor Novello! This is what John wrote, a small piece of theatre history:

'I remembered the time when our local theatre was the Everyman in Cheltenham. At that time the director had a collection of old-timers who he used quite often and among them was Cecily Courtneidge and, inevitably, Jack Hulbert. Cicely never just entered or left a room but she did so with a flourish, and often a brief pause with a glance at the audience, and she always had a round of applause on every entrance and exit! I remember too that on one occasion Jack Hulbert played a policeman – he was at least twenty years too old – and carried a clipboard, which obviously held his script. Cicely used to prompt him from time to time – 'Should we sit down and you can ask us some questions?' she would say. We loved it all! Happy memories.'

19 March

I am reading David Bentley Hart's recently published new translation of the Gospels. What emerges more clearly is Jesus' conviction that the end of the world was near, and that all who chose to follow him should give up all possessions, all their family. And so the early community, in expectation of the Second Coming in their own lifetime, gave away all their possessions. On other counts the teaching of Jesus is as strict as that of any Calvinist. Yet over the centuries his teachings have been watered down.

20 March

To the Royal Free for my massage, then some shopping and later in the evening I write some more pieces for my 2019 blogs. And now to bed, but at the weekend the clocks move forward and that will make a huge difference.

Today, however, was milder and so I did some work in the garden.

21 March

Today Jesus Christ comes to lunch. Well, it isn't everyone who can say that. He is coming in the person of Roger Hinde who in my 1973 production of the

*Chester Mystery Plays* played Christ. In one of my recent blogs I had quoted a note I had given him re: the way Jesus taught. 'The actor must be continually aware of the wider and deeper implications of each of Jesus' remarks, for like all Gnostic teachers, he sees things *sub species aeternitatis*. It is all too easy to take Jesus' remarks literally. Jesus does not bind people with rules and regulations but sets each person free to become the individual they are meant to be.'

This resulted in Roger writing to me:

'Dear James, I have just read your latest post. Prior to this I was just speaking to a friend about how you directed me in the role of Christ in the Chester Mystery Plays 1973. I am quite shocked by this strange coincidence. Now retired and resurrected from an aggressive and life-threatening cancer I love each day of my life – walking and writing. Your posts reflect the man I remember'. He then writes the following:

'STEPPING HILL HOSPITAL, September 2010.

This is my dying bed. I am only connected to the world by tubes, drips and catheters, blue-flesh inserts and plasters. I am isolated in a white side ward with white walls, a white ceiling and a grey outlook over a demolished factory. The morphine left me some days ago. One of my kidneys has been removed, my bladder, my prostate, my lymph glands. As I struggle to move in my dirty bed I catch sight of my unhealed wounds. I resemble an untidy counter in a butcher's shop. It is cemetery quiet this Sunday evening in the hospital. There is a knock on my door. 'Come in!' I say weakly. Before me stands a man. He had a look about him that I had only ever seen in one other human being. That was James Roose-Evans. The man who had entered my room shone like Jesus. 'You're a religious man, aren't you?' I said and although I was making a statement he answered 'I am.' In the depths of my despair I knew my Saviour had arrived. He wore no uniform. He came to my bedside and took my hand. In a quiet warm voice he said 'I have come to tell you that you are not going to die – I am going to pray for you and you will get better.'

I thanked him and wept as I am doing now in recalling this. The 'Jesus' man (was it him?) left after about fifteen minutes. From that moment I did get better, little by little, day by day. Recovery was a long and difficult road but now I am fully alive and creative again.

Dear James, I haven't seen you for 36 years but in that time I have thought about you many times. You are an inspiration, a shining light.

I feel like the Prodigal Son. Perhaps you can use my story to give hope and strength to others. Thank you for your posts. In appreciation and with great affection, from a Christ of 1973, Roger Hinde.'

At 12.15 Roger arrives, exuding a robust good health, and brimming with warmth, creativity, affection, bubbling with ideas – it is indeed a kind of Resurrection! He is a man who truly celebrates life each moment and each day. When he leaves I work on my Blogs for next year, and complete eight, which leaves me with sixteen more to go. I have to wait for ideas to bubble up from the inner spring! But I also find old notebooks with quotes, as well as private jottings such as this one that I wrote to a friend, 'My restless spirit is contained within a nave of silence.'

22 MARCH

I go to visit Estelle Spottiswoode, who sleeps, her mouth a gaping dark hole. It is a slow dying. I sit with her for fifteen minutes, praying. Back here with shopping for Sunday's lunch. On the final page of Thomas F.O'Meara's book *Vast Universe* I find this quote from a book by Christian de Duve entitled *Life Evolving: Molecules, Mind and Meaning*:

'We need priests – or better said, spiritual guides so as to avoid the pomp of robes and rites that surround the historical image of the priest – to serve as mentors who, without dogmatism or fundamentalism can inspire, help, and orient.' That indeed defines my own understanding of being a priest.


## 23 MARCH

Where has today gone! I spent the morning clearing endless papers – it is a day-by-day, week-by-week, month-by-month process! Shed, shed, shed!


## 24 MARCH

To the Royal Free for my annual blood-test for the Oncology department then to M&S to buy two pots of chives for the garden. The lodger is spending the day in the British Library, researching. Anne comes at 2 p.m. to give me my Alexander lesson.


## 25 MARCH

Nicola and her husband Christopher, Selina, and Frank to lunch here. My hearing aids were playing up so I had to strain to listen. Maybe I should emulate Evelyn Waugh and use an ear trumpet. I told the story, once recounted to me by Malcolm Muggeridge, how Waugh loathed him so, and once, when they were seated next to each other at a formal dinner party, he removed the ear trumpet and placed it on the table so that he wouldn't have to listen to Malcolm!

## 26 MARCH, MONDAY

To the ENT Hospital in Gray's Inn Road. Three weeks ago I was given a discharge by Dr Logan at the Tropical Diseases Hospital, my ear infection having healed. Today I waited an hour to be told I am discharged by the ENT hospital. On each visit to the ENT there are long waits, sometimes I have waited two hours. It is easy to see how overstretched the NHS is, which is such a valuable service, and how overworked the staff are. My friend Joan Dodman, who suffers from Myeloma and has to make frequent visits to the hospital for infusions, tells me her Consultant is retiring, she is too exhausted. Some 350 patients attend her clinic. It is clear that, as the population grows older, the hospitals are going to be even more crowded.

Back here to do some shopping and *The Times* Concise Crossword.

## 28 MARCH

Norman comes for a simple lunch and then drives me to the Garden Centre to buy compost, builder's sand, and liquid seaweed for the two olive trees in the front.

## 30 March, Good Friday

I find myself reflecting on the Resurrection and how when I was directing the *Chester Mystery Plays* in 1973 I went at one point to see Dean Addleshaw and asked him: What did Jesus wear at the Resurrection? I mean, what does the actor playing Jesus wear?'

'Dear me!' replied the Dean, 'I have never been asked that. Come back in three days after I have consulted my books.' After that symbolic space I returned to be told that he didn't know! As I was also working at that time with Malcolm Muggeridge I put the question to him. Without a moment's hesitation he replied, 'My dear boy, he was clothed in transcendental glory.'

Clearly the Resurrection was not a physical one. Not only would Jesus have been very weak from loss of blood, barely able to walk because of the wounds in his feet, and then where would he have found a suit of clothes, and where did he live during the forty days before he supposedly ascended into heaven? News would also have got out that he had not died, and the authorities would clearly have arrested him and executed him once and for all. It seems to me clear that so charismatic was his personality that it is perfectly understandable that he should have appeared as a vision to his close friends and followers. While not everyone has this experience after the death of a loved one, there are, nonetheless, countless stories of people who have.

And while I never 'saw' Hywel after his death, I have several times experienced his presence very closely. On one occasion I awoke in the small hours to feel his presence and laughter filling the room, which was pulsating with energy. He seemed closer than close, so that I, wide awake, called out, 'Hywel, you are amazing!'

That the women are said to have found the tomb empty except for the shroud is indeed possible – in Tibet it is known as 'the rainbow body'.

Indeed, in *The Tibetan Book of Living and Dying*, Sogyal Rinpoche says that a person who knows she or he is about to obtain a rainbow body will ask to be left alone and undisturbed for seven days. On the eighth only the hair and nails are found. There are many examples of this phenomenon and he describes that of Sonam Namgyal, a stone carver who was a hidden yogin. Just before his death at 79, he said, 'All I ask is that when I die don't move my body for a week.' On the eighth day when the undertakers came to take his body, when they undid the coverings (like Jesus' shroud) they found only his hair and nails.

31 March

Rain, rain, rain! But I have filled nine vases with daffodils by way of celebrating Easter, a delightful centrepiece invented by the lodger two Easters ago!

The lodger, to my delight, comes into the central

room to sit in an armchair and read… just this silent company is such a blessing. The more so on Easter evening, awaiting the Resurrection. How comforting it is to have his presence in the room rather than being on my own.

# APRIL 2018

1 APRIL

My blog for today is so central to my belief in the importance of friendship that I want to quote it here. It is entitled Relationships:

'I recently came across a review I wrote for *The Tablet* of the last book by Michael Mayne, the former Dean of Westminster Abbey. In 2005 he was faced with a diagnosis of cancer of the jaw which would, he realised, test his deepest beliefs.

Throughout his illness his wife Alison was his constant companion and it is this that leads him to write most movingly about all committed relationships, including same-sex relationships. He quotes from William Blake: 'We are put on earth that we may learn to bear the beams of love.' In such relationships we become, he says, the occasion for each other's self-realisation, for ultimately it is through one another and in each other that we may be entitled at the last to say, as God in the burning bush said, "I am who I am".

## 2 APRIL

Rain and cold persist! I have been pondering the matter of synchronicity, how certain encounters, events, even a book opened at a certain passage, seem pre-planned. But if we are constantly surrounded by noise we shall miss many of these moments. To give but one example: the way in which suddenly, out of the blue, we find ourselves thinking about someone we haven't heard from, or had contact with, for quite a time. Always, I believe, one should act on this and get in touch with that individual. Time and again, we find that the person has been thinking of us and wanting to make contact, having perhaps a need to share some problem or anxiety. It is in the same way that some individuals turn up in our lives just when we need them.

It is now nearly 4 p.m. and I have had an hour's nap, I did not get up until half past ten, yet I seem to need a lot of sleep. And if this is to be an honest account of my 91st year then I have to admit I am feeling my age, aware that I tire much more easily, and limbs ache. I also observe how, when eating, my hand shakes as I lift food on a fork and it falls off! But I don't talk about this or burden others with it. I also observe the constant ache, day and night, from my hernia, which cannot be operated on because of my age and even if it were, there is no guarantee, says Jonathan, my doctor, that it would be righted. So I wear a surgical belt and get on with it and tell no one. No boring organ recitals for my friends.

3 April

I was lying in bed, having again retired early – well, 9 p.m. – when the phrase 'existential loneliness' came into my head, so I got up and googled to find the exact meaning. It is frequently caused by not having a clear role carved out for one. If one is sure of one's place in life, if one's role is clearly defined, then one doesn't feel one is apart.

While I continue to miss Hywel's physical presence, the loneliness goes deeper; it is because I have no clearly defined role any more. I am a yesterday's man. Once I had a reputation as a director, as a writer, as a performer, but now in old age I no longer have a clearly defined role, though I am fortunate that I can write.

So for vast numbers of older people there is this deep sense of loneliness as they no longer have a clearly defined role in life. Yet I must remind myself of the occasion when I was visiting my friend Ann Powell, in her nineties, 'I wish I could do something!' she said and

I replied, 'Ann, you don't have to do anything. You are, and it is a joy just to be with you.'

She perfectly exemplified Emily Dickinson's poem 'A Perfected Life':

The props assist the house
Until the house is built,
And then the props withdraw-
And adequate, erect,
The house supports itself;
Ceasing to recollect
The augur and the carpenter.
Just such a retrospect
Hath the perfected life,
A past of plank and nail,
And slowness – then the scaffolds drop
Affirming it a soul.

I have lived such a rich life, as actor, director, writer, teacher, priest, that I now need to learn simply to be here as and when people need me, responding to whatever needs they bring one. So at my age, it is appropriate to let go of a lot of baggage, to accept that one's days of busyness are coming to a close, and to prepare for the eventual departure on the next stage of one's journey. While there is less outer work, there is still much inner work to be done!

The proofs of *A Shared Life* have arrived and I print

them off so that I can go through them line by line. Mariusz calls to install a new bulb over my desk, and another in the oven. He always refuses to take any money but I force an envelope into his pocket! He called out of the blue on Saturday bearing rich Polish cakes for Easter, and I gave him a great hug.

4 APRIL

Thinking about existential loneliness, and having no defined role, suddenly reminded me of the chapter in *Elsewhere and the Gathering of the Clowns*, the third in my sequence of Odd and Elsewhere books. Elsewhere is seated in the caravan of the King of the Clowns who tells him he is soon to retire and plans to name Elsewhere as his successor.

'Why do you have to retire?' asks Elsewhere. 'Why can't you go on being King?'

'It's time for me to retire. It will be the same for you one day; you will just know when the time has come. Besides, there's a new generation of clowns coming up and they will need a leader who is perhaps closer to them than I am.'

'What will you do when you retire?'

'I don't know yet. The moment one ceases to be King one no longer has power.'

What, of course, he will have is influence.

So there it is in a nutshell!

## 5 April

To the Royal Free for my massage. In some months Keith Hunt will be retiring from 55 years working at the Royal Free and is dreading it. He is very aware of what I shared with him about existential loneliness, about having no discernible role. At present, as he has done for decades, he gets up at 4 am and cooks a full breakfast, then drives to town and is at the hospital from 5.30 till 2 pm. He is often needed that early for patients going into the operating theatre and who are tense with nerves.

In the evening to the Savile Club for Norman's 70th birthday dinner party, at which I had to say the grace and later propose a toast. I was seated next to Josephine, Princess, Loewenstein; she is modest, warm and generous.

I was nearly late as in the cab I realised the battery of one of my hearing aids had gone, so I asked the driver to turn round and go back! But we made it to the Savile Club nonetheless on time! Phew!

## 6 April

This morning in to John Bell and Croyden to have a truss fitted for my umbilical hernia.

I have made some lentil soup, and am baking a loaf of wholemeal bread.

8 April, Sunday

Today Mary and her husband Andrew and their daughter Celia (not their real names) plus two friends arrive for the simple ritual I have devised to mark the end of their marriage. It all unfolds very naturally.

Two months ago Mary came to tell me that her husband was insisting on a divorce after 49 years. The circumstances around this were very painful when discovered and she was heart-broken. She asked me to devise a simple ritual that would mark the ending of their relationship. For several weeks I reflected and finally came up with a format but I insisted that their daughter Celia, now in her mid-thirties, plus two friends should be present.

I invited them to sit at the long table in my conservatory, and while holding hands, their eyes closed, to listen to Samuel Barber's 'Adagio for Strings', and to reflect on all the good things in their marriage, the many blessings and shared experiences, without any resentment for past failures or misunderstandings, and for their daughter to reflect on all the good things her parents had brought her.

Then began the simple ritual with Andrew holding Mary's hand that had the wedding ring and while removing it saying, 'I, Andrew, who gave you this ring to symbolise our marriage, now withdraw it by way of acknowledging that we are no longer husband and wife.'

Mary then said, 'I, Mary, accept that I am no longer your wife and that our task is to move on, with gratitude for all the good things we have shared.' Andrew then turned to their daughter, saying, 'Celia, I give you this ring for you to keep as a symbol that, although Mary and I are no longer husband and wife, we remain your parents and will always be there for you whenever there is need, and nothing can take that away.'

There was a pause, and Celia, reaching out to hold both her parents' hands, said, 'I love you both'. She then lifted her flute and played the Shaker hymn, *Simple Gifts*, which is all about learning to yield, to let go: 'till by turning, turning, we come round right'.

Two days later each wrote to say thank you and Mary in her letter wrote, 'I am both enriched and grateful. It was so powerful and simple. Until we did the ritual I didn't fully understand Celia's part. Now I see clearly the importance of her keeping my ring for I was distraught at the thought of just removing my ring and leaving it in a drawer when the divorce came through. It gives me consolation that she is keeping the ring safe. It feels right. That ring represented my complete trust in Andrew's love and support for me, but after all the revelations it felt as if it were a lie on my finger. But it still symbolises for me what was the truth for many years, the fact my trust in Andrew was fully justified: there was so much love between us for so long. Although I am hurt, grieving and angry, there will always be a part of me that loves him. I am still struggling with the impact of the revelations but I know that what you did for us last Sunday has been a huge step forwards into a new beginning. I felt released on Sunday. It was a roller coaster from grief to release.'

## 9 APRIL, MONDAY

To the dentist to see the hygienist and have my six monthly examination. No problems. I am lucky not to have dentures and still have a good head of hair.

## 10 APRIL, TUESDAY

Edward came to creosote the small garden study. I am also employing him weekly to move the heavy dustbins ready for collection, as tugging these heavy containers is not to be recommended for my hernia and I realised I must stop! I also arrange for Budgens to deliver my groceries instead of my lugging a heavy shopping trolley. I should have thought of all this ages ago.

I am also getting back into the habit of retiring later to bed, albeit the evenings are still darken too early, but I am also again, after a long absence, playing music on my CD machine. I have completed all my blogs for next year, twenty-four in all.

## 11 April

The great thing always to remember in any relationship is not to make demands. It is, of course, emotional insecurity that makes some people deeply possessive, as though afraid of being left alone. Loneliness is in the headlines today, in a report showing that while a large proportion of the older population live alone, it is the younger generation today that suffers most from loneliness. A new analysis has found that the highest rate of loneliness is found among those aged 25-34, of whom six per cent said that they always or often felt lonely. One in ten people aged between 16 and 24 say that they often or always feel lonely, compared with slightly more than one in 20 of all adults. The finding confounds assumptions that the elderly are most prone to loneliness. My impression is that loneliness is one of the chief factors in today's society. In the past there were street communities, religious communities of chapel, church and synagogue; in general people shared the same values and cared for each other. Sadly all this has fallen apart, which makes even a small group such as our meditation group an important oasis.

## 13 April

Sharon in to clean – I go shopping and make an appointment for next Tuesday to have my toenails cut.

I finish checking the final proofs of *A Life Shared*, and write captions for each of the photographs. I marinate chicken thighs in lemon juice, oil and tarragon and then cook in advance the Dublin Coddle for Ken who is coming to dinner on Sunday evening, so all I will have to do is heat it up.

14 APRIL

Little to report: shop, Alexander lesson, preparing food… but the sun shines, it is warm and one casts off extra garments. Has spring really arrived at last?

Evening: in facing the fact of existential loneliness I inch forward in that now I do not retire to bed until ten in the evening, and I drink only one glass of wine, whereas until recently I was prone to drinking several glasses to numb myself. All this as a result of that unexpected message from the unconscious, when the phrase 'existential loneliness' surfaced and I had no idea what it meant. We have but to listen!

15 APRIL, SUNDAY

Ken comes to supper and we have much sharing. On retiring to bed at eleven I find myself reflecting on the wisdom of the unconscious, and as with the dreams I had after Hywel's death, they well up from a deep part of one's unconscious and bring healing.

## 16 April

Because the expensive new hearing aids constantly play up I go to Amplifon in Wigmore Street to say I 'despair' and is there a chance of getting some of my money back?! Not only does the one in the right ear constantly scream but time and again I have to say to the lodger, or others, 'I can't hear what you are saying... let me go and put my old hearing aids back in,' and when I do, I hear everyone loud and clear.

Barry, the excellent audiologist, asks if he may try something else and does. The moment I arrive home and walk into the kitchen they start screaming, and the lodger, who is making a mug of tea, says 'I can hear them whistling.' So I ring Amplifon and make an emergency meeting at 3 p.m. tomorrow. In the morning I go to have my toenails clipped in England's Lane, and then at 2 p.m. Edward arrives to move out the bins for collection and do the first mow of the season. At 2 25 I go in a cab to Wigmore Street.

When I got home, the moment I entered the kitchen the right hearing aid began to scream loudly and again the lodger, making a pot of tea, could hear the whistling. Now the left one has also started screaming so I have made an emergency appointment for tomorrow, I think they are an expensive dead loss.

17 April

Have just made some tomato soup from a Waitrose recipe, and then I go off to Amplifon to sort out this hearing aid situation.

Barry Rogers at Amplifon accepts that the new hearing aids just aren't working for me and so I am to have a total refund! Amazing! That is well over £2,500!

I return singing the words – 'This is the weather the cuckoo likes – and so do I!'

18 April, 4 48 a.m.!

It is interesting how certain lines suddenly rise to the surface of one's memory, like yesterday recalling Hardy's line about 'this is the weather the cuckoo likes'. And now I wake up with words I haven't thought of for decades but clearly were meaningful in my troubled youth:

'Change around in all I see, but Thou who changest not, change me.'

I have had to water the garden, it is so hot! And I sing 'Summer is a-cumin in! – Loudly sing cuckoo!'

Singing these odd lines, all that I now remember, I think of other fragments from my childhood, especially certain lines from hymns, such as 'Guide me, O thou

Great Redeemer', which ends with the triumphal 'Land me safe on Canaan's side!' and then the evening hymn,

'The day Thou gavest, Lord, is ended,
The darkness falls at Thy behest...
The sun, that bids us rest, is waking
Our brethren 'neath the western sky
And hour-by-hour fresh lips are making
Thy wondrous doings heard on high.
Abide with me, fast falls the evening tide,
The darkness deepens, Lord with me abide.
When other helpers fail and comforts flee
Help of the helpless, oh abide with me.'

With a few exceptions, children no longer learn or sing these hymns for, as Mark Tully observed, we are no longer a Christian nation. Also lost are the rich treasures of games and rhymes children used to chant in the playground, which Peter and Iona Opie saved for posterity in their collection, *The Language and Lore of School-Children*. Now children are locked into their iPads.

Suddenly the clematis and other flowers are exploding into bloom and I have to water the garden, as the soil is so dry from the sudden heat wave.

## 20 April

Selina comes to tea in the garden and we share stories. She is such a relaxing and special friend. The lodger and I discuss possible places where he, Chris and I can spend five days, my first holiday in six or seven years. Anglesey was a possibility but he discovers that the average temperature at that time of the year can be 16 degrees, somewhat chilly. So we are looking at Landmark Trust properties in the south of England.

## 21 April

The lodger comes in to talk about existential loneliness, which he says can also be described simply as loss of role, something every out of work actor knows all too well. He reminds me how when we first met I had told him of when I was pushed out of Hampstead, without even a farewell party or gift. I was then in the wilderness for some time. But I came through all this. Change, as also in human relationships, requires soul work. Regarding change; I love this quote from Walt Whitman:

> 'Not I, nor anyone else, can travel that road for you.
> You must travel it by yourself.
> It is not far.
> It is within reach.'

Norman comes to supper but also bearing a new garden hose and he spends an hour fixing it to the wall outside. He does so much for other people. We discuss how both of us have this strong maternal side, which wants to help others, and give in different ways. The lodger is the same.

22 APRIL

Tony Morris arrives from Oxford to discuss progress on the publication of my latest book *A Life Shared*. We both share the same kind of energy and sense of fun! We sit out in the garden with pots of coffee, and when he leaves I load him up with more books to sell at Bleddfa, plus Victorian lace tablecloths. He has now suggested I should write a book on simple rituals.

23 APRIL

Thanks to the lodger's research we have found an idyllic cottage with a secret garden just a 15 minute walk from the centre of Rye. It looks so reminiscent of the Granary where Pick lived that I know I shall be content just to sit in the garden and read while he and Chris, who will also drive us, go off on jaunts on their own!

24 APRIL

I work on the new book about simple rituals.

25 APRIL

The day interrupted by Scottish Power coming to install a smart meter, which meant turning off all lights, and this involved lugging out bookcases to get at points, crawling under my desk, etc. all of which the lodger kindly did.

26 APRIL, 2 30 A.M.

In deep sleep, X comes and lies on my bed. Nothing is said but gently he presses his lips to mine. On waking I ponder these gifts that well up from the unconscious, something that will never happen in real life, and yet a strange kind of love and loving is at work deep down in one's psyche. I give thanks for such visitations.

I am reminded of a fragment of a 9th century poem, translated by Helen Waddell,

'By day mine eyes, by night my soul desires thee.
Weary I lie alone.
Once in a dream it seemed thou wert beside me;
O far beyond all dreams if thou would'st come!'

Noon: I have been reflecting on how many live, as it were, in houses where so many rooms are locked, which have never been entered, and where the shutters are closed so that no daylight penetrates. But if one is fortunate to go into analysis, then one begins to open these closed rooms. It is not for nothing that we have the expression 'skeletons in a cupboard'. I was fortunate to have had many years of Jungian analysis, and continue to have friends who are analysts and with whom I can discuss certain dreams. The experience of a 'true' analysis reveals the rich potential that is in each of us. Alas, so many are born millionaires but die in poverty, their full potential never realised.

I go to the Royal Free for my oncology check up and am to have a scan in two month's time.

## 27 APRIL

Another fragment of poetry has risen to my memory, which was used by Martha Graham in one of her works... the line is:

'Too late to be born to this instant – the cry of the god is upon us.'

How easily one can miss one's moment! As Hamlet says, 'the readiness is all'. Be ready to pack your bags and move on, here have we no dwelling place!

Old age is a preparation for an eventual departure to another country, and so one has to sort out one's belongings, keeping only the bare necessities for the journey ahead. It is also a time in which, as we lose friends, and whatever role we may once have had, we have to learn to stand alone. And yet I am moved to know how dearly I am loved by certain friends and that I am not alone, as countless millions are.

A message has come through via the Bleddfa website from Mathew Evans who writes, 'I was lucky enough to work for James in 1978. I was an assistant stage manager for a play called Mate. It was a comedy starring Britt Ekland, Rupert Penry-Jones, and Julian Holloway. It was not by any means a great play and we all knew it, but the show went on. James had the job of Sisyphus pushing this recalcitrant unfunny boulder up an endless slope towards its first night. He did it sweetly, generously, and joyfully, but it is hard work teaching a platypus to fly.

For rehearsals we had taken over the upstairs room of an old Victorian pub in the Tottenham Court Road. One afternoon James wanted to run the whole play, and wanted a vantage point to watch it from. He placed a tall bar stool high up on the bar, and sat on it to watch. Maybe he wanted to hide in the shadows. Halfway through the run I was distracted by James' ever-present lengthy scarf sliding gently and gracefully to the floor. Looking up I saw our leader a good dozen feet in the air, elegantly fast asleep in the shadows by the ceiling. How he stayed balanced up there I have no idea. But after his much needed snooze he gave the cast detailed notes on how to improve their performances and left for the day. Very cool.'

Of course I don't remember this incident but I do remember begging our producer to keep the show on the road but not bring it in to town. He brought it in to the Comedy Theatre where it died a predictable death!

To the Garrick with Melanie for the recital by the Kanneh-Mason Trio. It was sensational, and while the recitals usually end at 8 p.m., this went on, because of repeated cheers, until 8 15. The three were beaming with delight, the more so as Bruce Harris, who has masterminded these recitals so brilliantly over the past three or four years, told us their father was in the audience. Melanie tells me that there is a fine BBC documentary about this remarkable Afro-Caribbean family, all seven of whom are musicians. Being in the front row one is so aware of their own awareness of each other, listening acutely, looking at one another, smiling at certain moments. A complete unity.

## 28 April

Reading again Edward Edinger's book *The Christian Archetype – a Jungian commentary on the life of Christ*. In examining the Agony in the Garden he points out how the experience is plagued by sleepiness. Three of the four figures sleep through the whole event. The emphasis is on wakefulness for what is at issue is the birth of consciousness. The source of inner strength constellated by prayer or active imagination is personified in Luke by the ministering angel. As Jung wrote, 'The highest and most decisive experience of all is to be alone with one's inner self.' We must be alone if we are to find out what it is that supports us when we can no longer support ourselves.

There is a strong degree of synchronicity in my reading this now as I am still struggling with acute loneliness and a general sense of uselessness.

For each of us, right up to the very end, the work continues, allowing aspects of one's self to die so that new growth is possible. The life, death and Resurrection of Christ is an archetype of the inner journey that each of us is called upon to take.

29 APRIL

I work on the ritual book.

30 APRIL

I receive a very long email from Rowan Williams, first of all thanking me for sending him a copy of *Blue Remembered Hills – A Radnorshire Journey*, of which he writes;

'It was good to see how the Bleddfa vision developed – and good also to see how all of that provided a definition of the priestly identity that you inhabited, in ways that (sadly) not all that many these days seem to understand. Again and again as I read, I found myself deeply moved by this discovery of priestliness, and it gave me a lot to reflect on. You were fortunate to find a sympathetic bishop in that remarkable figure John Eastaugh, whom I met a couple of times. The lukewarm attitude of some other clerical colleagues, though, is sad to read about. But it did make me think that it's far too long since I visited Bleddfa and I must make time for this.'

He then goes on to analyse in detail the manuscript of my book *Holy Theatre: Rediscovering the Sacred in Worship*, which he read over Christmas 'with a lot of gratitude and resonance, and it seemed to me to be an important contribution in an area that's a bit of a desert'. He then goes on to give me very detailed and invaluable editorial comments so that now I can see where I need to edit and reshape, etc. It is incredibly generous of him. He concludes, 'The book seems too important not to see the light somehow.'

Charlie comes for coffee and deep good sharing re: the journey he is on, and shortly Piers Plowright will be here for tea. So not much writing today. The lodger has brought me as a gift a splendid cookbook, *The Pleasures of the Table* by Theodora Fitzgibbon.

# MAY 2018

## 1 May

Edward arrives to work in the garden and is now up a ladder trimming the pyracanthas hedge, which is growing too tall. At least the sun shines although it is quite cool. The lodger has to leave at 4 a.m. to catch his plane for the Canary Islands!!

## 2 May

The past two days I have been solidly working on the text of *Holy Theatre: Rediscovering the Sacred in Worship*, encouraged by Rowan Williams' very positive praise, as well as his detailed editorial feedback. As a result it is now a slimmer, tauter book.

To the Royal Free to see the hernia specialist

privately. I don't have an umbilical hernia as was diagnosed before, but it is the weakening of the stitches in the long cut made when I had two-thirds of my colon removed. He can't operate as I am on warfarin, but says go on wearing the truss, and with luck I should be OK.

In checking the china for the big party of 40 people here on Sunday week, the shelf collapsed and all the china fell on the floor! Much got broken. Tony who installed the cupboard is coming tomorrow to repair the shelf, and I need to buy twenty more bowls, etc. at least.

3 MAY

No hot water and no heating. Fortunately Tony is a plumber and so sorted out the problem. I go on the C11 bus to Finchley Road to pay my refund cheque from Amplifon into my deposit account at NatWest and on the way back I buy more spoons and bowls for the party. I hose the garden because of the sudden warmth, and it is just possible the first roses may be out in time for the party!

4 MAY

Sharon comes to clean and when I tell her I need to buy more dishes and spoons, she tells me to go to the big pound shop in Camden Town. So I get a cab there but no luck. However, on the street corner is a man with a stall selling fruit and vegetables, and I buy a bowl of five lemons for £1, and also one of four red peppers, also for £1. I then visit the Reject Shop near the Round House and buy 20 china bowls and 20 dessert spoons and the man says he will deliver them for me, as I daren't risk carrying such a heavy load.

I return to make a fresh supply of potato, leek and onion soup to go in the freezer, and tomorrow I shall cook the braised rabbit from a recipe in the Theodora Fitzgibbon cookbook. I am also going to follow her recipe for boiling a chicken in just fifteen minutes but with four silver-plated forks inside the bird! She was told of it by a Chinese cook and, incredible though it sounds, it works! I have also made two jars of tomato chutney from one of her receipts. Much of all this will go in the deep freeze.

5 MAY

Another day of summer, and I remove daffodil bulbs from the two large urns and plant out the boar geraniums I had ordered. How one's spirits lift in such weather.

# 6 MAY

My good friend Jenny writes to me about ageing (I had told her of my experience of existential loneliness) saying that such was clearly a major rite of passage in the adventure of ageing, and especially retirement from work. 'When I was winding up my psychotherapy practice, I attended a few meetings of a very interesting retirement group for members of the Westminster Pastoral Foundation where I trained. People talked about how they would miss their patients and the routines of practice, but then they began to enjoy having time for new things totally unrelated to our professions. These discoveries began to take over after a period of mourning the loss of role and the recognition that accompanies paid work.'

She then goes on to make this important observation: 'This kind of loss is going to become a very common experience for people of all ages as technology takes over huge swathes of the world of work. People will have to find more rewarding and less expensive things to do with their time and freedom than drink and drugs, which, understandably, now fill the gap for a lot of desperate people. These looming changes are going to require even bigger changes in politics and economics and the way society is organised, a process which hasn't even begun.'

## 7 May

Sorting out of papers is seemingly endless. I come across a fascinating account of my meeting with the French star Geneviève Page in 1970 when I was running Stage Two, the experimental wing of the Hampstead Theatre. She had heard about our work and asked to meet me at the Carlton Towers Hotel where she was staying. Tall and slim, wearing an apple green corduroy suit with a sleeveless sheepskin jerkin, her blonde hair cut short, and her golden eyes that seemed to have a green centre, she was the most beautiful woman I had ever met. She looked like the young David about to slay Goliath!

She made me sit beside her on the sofa as she curled up at one end. She told me she was married to a severe, formal Frenchman who had tried to model her according to what he wanted of her, with the result that she went dead inside. She has two children, aged five and six. Why is she telling me all this?

Although she suffers from vertigo she loves to ski, reciting her roles aloud on the steepest slopes, shouting her words out to the mountains. She speaks about the need for muscle when playing tragedy.

The room grows dark as we talk. The sun sets and lights come on in the houses in the square, but she does not get up to switch on the lights. She telephones Paris to enquire after the children. She speaks in Spanish to the manservant to say she will not be back that evening.

Then William Wyler, the film director, telephones. She is to be in a Sherlock Holmes film for him with Robert Stephens and Colin Blakely. She was to have done Edward Albee's *Tiny Alice* in London with Maximilian Schell, she tells me, but Michael White, the producer, was unable to raise the money. It is the part she most wants to play.

As the sun sets there are spirals of smoke in the sky. Church towers and spires are silhouetted against its deepening blue. As the room darkens with shadow, so her face looks older, and her anxieties and stresses show themselves more. She quotes from André Gide: 'La difficulté, ce n'est pas choisir, mais eliminir'. She also says, 'Is it Einstein who says you never meet a wise man with a serious face?'

She is so beautiful and I don't know what to do. I am aware that, seated in the dusk, having been talking for six hours, we are very close. Ever so close. She says, 'Shall we have supper sent up to us?' This throws me, my mind begins racing, and I don't know how to cope. Clearly she wants me to stay longer, to stay the night. I have never been with a woman and would not know what to do, yet do find her so irresistibly attractive. I find myself inventing an excuse, I tell her that I must leave as I have an appointment with our choreographer, Yoma Sasburg, at Stage Two.

And I never saw her again, and yet our meeting haunts me still, with the memory of that slim, boyish, golden figure curled up beside me in the dusk, with all her inner pains.

## 8 MAY

When I came here I placed at the end of this long garden a tall mirror, eight feet high by four feet in width, which reflects the garden. This morning I woke at about five to see the mirror full of orange-golden lights like baubles on a Christmas tree – the mirror was reflecting the rising sun, but I could not understand why it was like so many blobs until I realised that the sun was being filtered through the leaves of an overhanging branch. When I woke again at half past six, the mirror now was full of bright silver ornaments, sparkling. There are compensations in waking early. It was 8.45 and I was still in my pyjamas, running the bath when the doorbell rang, and I thought, oh, another delivery. But it was Gabriel and his assistant coming to clean the windows. I thought that was tomorrow. I do sometimes get days muddled.

## 9 MAY

I am deeply immersed in reading afresh Vikram Seth's novel *An Equal Music*, which is beautifully written and so moving in its portrait of a frustrated love.

## 10 May

Edward comes in the morning for three hours to trim the hedges in the front, mow both lawns, and do some weeding.

I simmer the remains of the chicken to make stock, and then shall add it to the vegetables I am cooking to make chicken soup.

I write a long letter to Vikram Seth. The last time we met was at the internment of Michael Mayne's ashes in Westminster Abbey, and the first (and only other time) we met was when Hywel and I were staying with Peter and Anne Simor in their house overlooking a weir. Vikram was studying pottery with Peter and, like us, stayed overnight. At breakfast the next morning when we were sitting on the terrace drinking tea and eating toast and marmalade, Vikram appeared with a large glass of red wine and some of the cold meat from the previous evening's dinner!

Dan comes to help me with a computer problem and then I spend the rest of the evening addressing 144 envelopes ready to send out invitations to the launch party of my next book, *A Life Shared*.

## 11 May

One of the central characters of Vikram's novel is the musician Julia who becomes stone deaf and so can no longer play with other musicians, or engage in telephone conversations, being totally dependent on lip reading. This is one of the most haunting aspects of this remarkable novel and reveals how deeply isolating this must be for such a person. I can partially relate to this as, with age, my hearing is impaired but helped by good hearing aids. But in general the level and quality of speech today has declined so that frequently on the telephone I have to say to someone, you are speaking too fast, or too softly or, as is increasingly frequent today speaking with a thick accent. I very much doubt whether elocution is taught nowadays.

12 MAY

Still sorting papers I come across a small paper I wrote about a remarkable woman, Marie Mathias, which was published as the first of a series of Bleddfa Papers, and entitled 'Marie's Orchard', being her story in her own words. It was in 1988 that she first began writing to me when she was in her late eighties, after having heard me on television. I responded and she began to send me her dreams and our friendship grew through this correspondence until eventually we met.

After a series of falls which necessitated her moving into a nursing home and selling her bungalow in Chichester, she wrote less and telephoned more, sometimes late in the evening when she was often frightened, bewildered and unhappy. I encouraged her to telephone whenever she wished, however late.

In September 1989 she was the first person to respond to an appeal by the Bleddfa Trust to purchase some barns, two fields, and an orchard, which make up what is now the Barn Centre. I was so moved by her generous response that I wrote to tell her we were naming the orchard Marie's Orchard. Earlier that year, on 22 June 1989, a week before her ninetieth birthday she wrote to me, 'I wait for life to unfold and hope to go with it.' Increasingly over her last years she learned to listen to the voice of what she referred to as 'the Guardian within'. 'My inner guidance reminds me we are all members of one another, interdependent in the oneness, and how very important it is to be constantly in touch with the deepest, innermost self.' Marie remained questing and questioning to the end.

She wrote to me, in her first letter;

'I watch little TV, distrust fantasy; belong to no established church, find both prayer and worship in the usual sense difficult; I have meditated, seedless and silent, since about 1942, and have been hooked on dreams in a big way since then, they are more meaningful than ever, and so is my zest for life.

In 1970 my husband died. In the following two years, two nervous breakdowns gave me hell, but I would not wish to have missed them. Although disabled, I now live alone and revel in my aloneness. Many young and youngish friends are very good to me while a small group of Jungian orientated friends gather weekly here for a talk and a meditation. Yes, indeed, old men and old women need to be explorers. At present I am exploring Death, at times exciting and thrilling, at times deeply sad and tragic too – and scaring!'

In other letters she continued to share her reflections:

'Eight years ago, Dr Gordon Starte, a Jungian, took me on. The work we are doing is helping me face my shadow side. Slowly I am changing and coming to the point of truly saying 'Thy will, not mine, be done.' My constant prayer is: Lord, teach me, guide me, use me. Yes, yes, yes, to you for saying we cannot be overwhelmed by God, only fulfilled. That does away with the fear, doesn't it? Awareness grows that in some way you are leading me to a clearer understanding of God in the depths of my being, deeper than ever before. A strange thought has come to me, out of the blue. The choice comes to tell you or not? The 'amazing to me' thought is that you are being the mother I longed for and never had! You have listened to my story, you have nourished me, giving me time and thought. Are you helping me to become who I am? No wonder I sobbed.

'I am learning to accept my weaknesses and not to worry about my failings. I know that this is part of myself that needs to change. This comes about by watching my response to what happens. If it is negative, I must make the effort to be more positive in thought, word and action. I need to be aware that I am not alone; healing forces are all around me.

My interest in Bleddfa, your Centre for Caring and the Arts, and its future, belong to a far-seeing part of me. I felt a bit shaken when in your letter you referred to 'Marie's Orchard'. It stirs my depths and makes me cry.'

My need for you is to help me die well, and that is being able to let go of the weak and frightened me. Better still, to take her in my arms and love her. On my inner journey I have heard the words, 'Dissolve in the formless.'

Marie's acceptance of old age and preparation for death is a wonderful example of what each of us should be doing as we age. But I think also of the increasing number of young people today, in their mid-twenties, dying of cancer, as Keith Hunt at the Royal Free Hospital informed me, as well as the increase of suicides among young men in particular. Who is there to help them?

Sometimes I am asked: Do you believe in an afterlife? Way beyond belief, even though I have no evidence, I am in no doubt that there is continuity beyond this life. But I don't think it will be like the end of a Hollywood movie, that two people will be together forever and ever!

I am convinced we shall know one another, but we shall all have tasks, other lives to lead, other work to do.

13 May

The lunch party from 2 p.m. – 6 p.m., a great success! Fortunately the sun shone and so everyone was able to gather in groups in the garden.

14 May

Everything back to normal. But the vases of magnificent peonies, slightly tinged with pink like a faint blush, and azaleas, with eucalyptus leaves, remind one how splendid it all looked, and what a luxury such flowers are, here in the centre room, in the conservatory, in the hall and in the passageway.

I go to have tea with my friend R, who has been having a very painful bereavement over the past five or so years since her husband died. Today, however, in spite of being physically more frail, she is able to tell how, during their sixty years of marriage, they often had blazing rows and once she even threw herself on the floor. All very Ibsen! But because they loved each other, they persevered, which is why I hope that my book, *A Life Shared*, will speak to straight readers as well as gay, about how, in a long relationship, it is important to work through the many vicissitudes without screaming divorce!

## 17 May

There is an email from the Keats Group Practice saying the blood tests I had done yesterday reveal a high level of potassium, which affects the kidneys, and explains why I am in acute pain, almost crippling. My telephone however has broken down and so I grab a black cab and go to the surgery where they give me a form for a fresh blood test, which I shall have at 11-tomorrow morning. I google for information about high levels of potassium and discover among forbidden foods some I have been gorging down, such as 20 or so spring onions each day, marmite on biscuits, drinking Worcester sauce from the bottle! So I print off all the information and plan to reorganise my eating habits.

I make some Carrot and Orange soup from a recipe of Theodora Fitzgibbon, and marinate some chicken legs.

## 18 May

To the surgery for another blood test. I finish reading *The Garden Party* by Elizabeth Taylor. She always avoids always clichéd endings, a neat tidying up. You realise that the characters will just continue to muddle along. I have ordered Nicola Beauman's biography *The Other Elizabeth Taylor*.

## 19 May

Anne comes to give me my Alexander lesson, then Dan and a friend who have been walking on the Heath drop by, and we sit in the garden drinking water and cordial, and gossiping. Anne says I need only water the pots, which, as my back is causing me a lot of pain in the kidney area, is a great relief. Tomorrow Rupert comes to breakfast at 9.30 after attending Mass at St Dominic's, and then the lodger and I shall share a pork with prunes casserole I have cooked.

## 20 May

The pain became so excruciating last night that I cancelled Rupert coming to breakfast, and, encouraged by the lodger, rang emergency as, whether walking, standing, sitting or stooping (unable to get into the bath) the pain had become excruciating. Two lady doctors arrived, did thorough tests, blood pressure, urine, etc. all fine and it is not the kidneys but my right hip. They tell me to take 8 paracetamol a day and they will arrange an x-ray of the hip, and that I should go for the third blood test tomorrow, and go on drinking water, as the lodger urged, but which I had almost stopped doing after reading the diet chart for this condition. Already as a result of the paracetamol the pain is less. Phew! I really was crippled with pain, quite alarming.

Sorting through yet more old papers I come across a fragment I wrote long before I met Hywel but which anticipated *A Life Shared*:

'This meeting has been planned from the beginning of time. We are united forever now in an eternity of acceptance. We shall be the crossroads from which life will flow out to people. You do not yet know me though I have long turned to you. The dark places that lie in each of us we accept. We walk in darkness but are full of light.'

As I wrote in *Opening Doors and Windows* of my first meeting with Hywel, 'how do two people manage to be in the same place at a particular moment and had they missed that moment would they have remained strangers?' As John O'Donohue writes in *Eternal Echoes*, 'There is a whole area of secret preparation and gathering here that we cannot penetrate with our analytical or conscious minds.' As Hywel always said, 'We were meant to meet'. And that is true also of other relationships, including that with the lodger.

Reflecting on the above I recall how when I was sixteen and a Rover Scout I organised a summer camp for about 20 scouts, and we were joined by two French scouts from Paris, Pierre aged 18 and Francois my age, both intending to become priests. There were eight of us in my bell tent, each in our sleeping bags. On the first night, as we settled down into our bags, I said to Francois, who was next to me, in French, as he spoke no English, 'Might I sleep with my hand in yours?' and he nodded. In the middle of the night I woke the entire camp with a great cry of desolation. I was on my knees, howling, because Francois' hand had slipped out of mine, and I was bereft. I didn't fully understand this at the time but later, on reflection, I realised that my whole boyhood had been dominated by my mother's restlessness which meant I attended some sixteen schools. We lived in many more homes for, like a gypsy, she loved moving. The result was that I was never able to put down any roots or form any friendships.

O'Donohue writes that the hunger to belong is at the heart of our natures. It is in our natures to long for companionship and even more so today in our fragmented society. A recent news report is of a considerable number of individuals even in their forties who have never been able to form relationships; while, as I have already recorded, more than 50 per cent of first marriages end in divorce in the fourth or fifth year.

21 May

To the Royal Free for a third blood test, then on the C11 bus to Waitrose to buy cod loin and halibut. The lodger rings to ask how I am and to say he won't be back till 10 p.m. I shall cook my piece of halibut with herbs, butter and white wine, in foil, and eat it along with a salad.

## 22 MAY

The sun shines, Edward comes to work in the garden. Out on the front lawn is the pine desk from the lodger's room, waiting to be collected by the Heart Foundation. To protect it from the rain a white sheet is laid over it so that it resembles an altar.

At 1 40 I leave to have a 24-hour heart monitor fixed at the Royal Free. I am cooking supper tonight for the lodger and myself.

Mike Williams has just been and persuaded me not to order a new laptop but a proper computer, and the larger screen which will be easier on my eyes etc.

At dusk I sit out in the garden watching the wind ruffling the curls of the trees, violently shaking their leaves. Hywel and I used to love walking in the woods at dusk, hearing the rattle of birds beginning to roost for the night. The topmost leaves are yellow green, catching the last light of the setting sun, while those lower down are a dark green. As in a striptease one has glimpses of the branches and limbs of each tree.

## 23 MAY

Shortly I shall be returning the heart monitor to the Royal Free, and tomorrow I am to have one more blood test, re: the level of potassium, and then see Dr Radia at 4, while at 12 30 Ruth and Nicholas come to lunch.

I have prepared the vegetables in advance, and taken out from the deep freeze the chicken pie, plus the carrot and orange soup which I shall serve cold. I have booked a cab to take me to the surgery at 10 a.m., to pick up a blood test form and then the cab will take me to the Royal Free. A busy day it will be.

## 24 MAY

The carrot and orange soup, à la Theodora Fitzgibbon, with crème fraiche and chopped coriander, is a real treat. Nicholas brings a large magnum of prosecco and we have drinks in the garden before lunch. In the afternoon I see Dr Radia and the potassium level in my blood has gone back to normal but I am to observe a special diet.

## 25 MAY

The computer arrives at 8 05. Mike Williams comes to set it all up. He has amazing patience and must have been a wonderful teacher. It is going to take me some time to adjust to the various changes required, and he is coming again tomorrow morning. Leap and the net will appear – indeed! Tomorrow I shall make more of Theodora Fitzgibbon's splendid tomato chutney, and prepare the Sunday evening supper for Norman who rang last night to say the new production of *84 Charing Cross Road* was well received in Darlington.

## 26 May

Mike Williams pays a second visit to continue setting up my new computer. I cook and bottle the tomato chutney and Celia drops by bearing white socks she has ordered for me, and we have a quiet talk seated in the arbour in the last of the sun. Because of potassium in the blood I am not supposed to drink much wine, if any, but the diet chart says OK for gin, whisky and rum. It is decades since I had a gin and tonic so I buy a bottle of each, and pour one level of gin to four of tonic water, plus ice and lemon, and drink four glasses, as it seems to have no effect. But then it suddenly hits me! I retire early to bed. That puts an end to gin!

## 27 May

The lodger produces a full Irish breakfast with bacon, sausages, egg, black pudding, white beans and fried tomato. I sit in the garden to meditate until it begins to spot with rain. But the roses are all in bloom, including the Ispahan.

## 28 May

A day lost!

## 29 May

At 9 a.m. two Polish workmen arrive to start removing the big bay window at the front, and the bars, replacing it with double-glazing. They work till seven in the evening. I spend the greater part of the day finishing reading Nicola Beauman's impressive biography of the writer Elizabeth Taylor, and she is organising for me a set of Elizabeth Taylor's books. After a night of lightning and thunder the heavens open and rain drenches down.

## 30 May

These two workmen, one Polish, one Estonian, are so thorough, hard working and courteous. It is a major upheaval and so somewhat distracting but the double-glazing will make such a difference to the lodger's room.

## 31 May

I go for another blood test and then Dr Radia pops in to see me to say that Dr Rakhit, the heart specialist, thinks my dizziness and uncertainty on my feet this past week may be due to my being on Ramopril and has suggested a change of medication which I start tomorrow.

Sorting yet more papers I come across the following account of when Ann Powell, then in her mid 90s, was in the cottage hospital at Kington and I used to visit daily and sit for two hours at a time, just being 'totally present'.

'I sit for two hours with Ann in her room at the Garth Nursing Home in Kington. These days she lies prone on her back, the rails up for safety.

Occasionally she eats a strawberry or a cherry or drinks water, but eats no other food. Her second kidney has given up and it is a matter of time. The doctor, in conjunction with Evelyn Bally, her cousin, has agreed she will be given morphine when the pain commences.

She is asleep when I arrive but opens her eyes and sees me. I say that I have been away for three days. 'In London?' she asks, then closes her eyes and goes back to sleep. I sit, holding her hand, and keep watch. That is all I can do, be totally present. There are occasional tremblings of her hands, her face, murmurs and sighs, and I think of the line from King Lear: 'We must endure our going hence'. Then she sinks into a deeper sleep and her frown disappears, her face becoming serene. At intervals she opens her eyes briefly and then closes them, as though disappointed to find herself still in this world. Outside the telephone rings from time to time, and there is the sound of someone hoovering, and the voices of the kitchen staff and the smell of cooking. Occasionally she opens her eyes wide – they are a deep bluebell colour, and she smiles at me. Then she closes them again. I feel privileged just to be able to sit here, keeping watch, being totally present, without any need for words. Once or twice she tightens her grip on my hand. Then she suddenly rings the bell for the nurses and two appear to deal with her bowel movement.

How long does it take to die? I wonder. When I arrive, passing along a corridor, I see that the doors to other rooms are always kept open. In one is an old man in a chair, curled sideways, embryonically, fast asleep. It is the same each time I come. In another a man lies in his bed, eyes closed, always the same, quite still, yet his television is on.

I think back to the time when I was directing a production of Michael Frayn's *Donkeys' Years* and each evening I would visit Aileen Dance, then 89, who had been an actress in Sir Frank Benson's company, but had had a bad fall and knew she would never return home and indeed died at the Royal Free Hospital.

On one of my visits she said, 'I feel I am coming to the end of a very long journey' and I replied, 'Yes, I think you probably are.'

'I lie here quite contented and peaceful,' she continued. 'They come and do all sorts of things to me, medicines and foods, but I feel it is a waste of time. It isn't necessary, it isn't necessary at all.' Later on she said, 'I know that when the moment comes it will be very simple. You will be there. I shall look up at you and then close my eyes.' Which is indeed what eventually happened. Then she added, 'Now there is nothing and no one' – said very simply. And I replied, 'Nothing but a great Love that surrounds you and me and all of us always,' to which she responded, 'and you convey that more than anyone. Where did you get your gift of friendship?'

# JUNE 2018

## 1 JUNE

Increasingly it seems to me that the source of all wisdom and the direction in our lives is contained within the Unconscious, that this is where we find God, the Divinity that shapes our ends, or Providence – whatever name we use. I have come to realise that letting go of all the roles I have played in my life, and just being, is what in old age my task is – simply to be!

## 2 JUNE

I have just come away from a funeral service that depressed me – so much of it was just bad theatre, such as people not projecting their voices, not knowing how to use a microphone. And the language so dated!

## 3 June, Sunday

Lisa gives the talk at our monthly meditation meeting about the meaning of courage, the central word 'cor' meaning heart, and so to have courage means opening our hearts and allowing ourselves to be vulnerable.

## 4 June

Because of a change in my medication I have had the most severe dizziness, and on Saturday had to ring for an emergency doctor. This morning, Jonathan, my own doctor rang, has spoken with Dr Rakhit, the heart specialist, and my medication is being changed. I have stopped the new medicine I had been prescribed and gone back on Digoxin and already feel better, though not yet out of the woods.

## 5 June

My new medication has arrived and I have started taking it. At the moment everything is a struggle and I swear at inanimate objects. I am hoping I shall be more on top of things by the time Norman drives us to Wales on Saturday.

## 6 June

Not so much dizziness but a tightening of the chest when walking, so going to the shops is a slow and exhausting process.

## 7 June

Edward comes to mow the grass and plant out sweet williams and some lilies. The day very close.

## 8 June

I go for a further blood test, then start preparing the picnic for tomorrow's journey. A box containing paperbacks of all the novels by Elizabeth Taylor arrives, organised by Nicola Beauman.

## 9 June

Norman drives me to Wales. It takes five hours but on arrival at Pilleth Oaks we are warmly welcomed by Heather Hood and given tea on a terrace overlooking fields full of sheep and their lambs. In the evening we dine with Peter Conradi in his amazing eyrie at Cascob, overlooking a small valley. Knackered by the long journey I sleep deeply.

## 10 June

Pilleth Oaks is such a comfortable guesthouse, full of beautiful china, ceramics and old furniture. After breakfast we drive to Bleddfa. People are already assembling and then at 11 o'clock Tony Morris leads me into the Hall Barn, where I am to have a conversation with the audience asking me any questions they choose. I have never been so nervous!

At the end I sound the deep bell for a ten minute silence, after which I quote Hamlet's 'There's a Divinity that shapes our ends, rough hew them how we will,' and then add 'there is a pattern and purpose to each life.'

In the foyer I sit at a table as people queue to buy my books, asking me to write in them. So many faces from the past, it is deeply moving, including a man I didn't know who was a small boy at Dolassey Farm and he remembers the night when I walked past and stopped, as he and his brother were feeding newborn lambs, which I describe in *Blue Remembered Hills*.

The Centre was looking so pristine, the grass in the orchard, and in the field below, smoothly mown, and down at the Old School Gallery a very impressive art exhibition. Then after a bowl of soup we set off back to London, hitting all the heavy traffic. Five hours later we are back.

## 11 JUNE

While the new medication I am taking has removed
the giddiness, I am finding walking more difficult,
a tightening in the chest, hips aching and having to
pause every fifteen yards or so. I walk now uncertainly
like a very old man!

## 12 JUNE

Phew! Lucie and Amelia from the Hampstead Theatre
come with Graham, cameraman and all his equipment to
film me talking about the early years of the Hampstead
Theatre Club. They seemed very pleased with the results.
It is for a film marking the 60th anniversary of the theatre
next September, and all the directors who succeeded me are
also being interviewed. Amelia Cherry revealed that Ann
Harvey is her grandmother. Ann is in charge of the Eleanor
Farjeon estate and Amelia grew up knowing all Eleanor's
books and wanted me to share my memories of Eleanor
who was also the first patron of the Hampstead Theatre
Club. I owe so much to the generosity of her friendship. It
was also Eleanor who, having read the first draft of a novel
I had written, sent it to her publisher at Methuen's, and she
came with me to meet him. He said that at 30,000 words
it was too short, but if I would write it to the traditional
length, they would seriously consider it for publication.

Three or four years later, having done this, I gave it to

Eleanor to read and she had to tell me that in the rewriting I had lost so much of the quality she had admired. It was a salutary lesson and made me realise that while I can write, I am not a novelist. She told me later how much it had cost her for, she said, 'You were like the son I might have had, and I didn't want to hurt your feelings and yet I could not do otherwise than be truthful.' To this day I am indebted to being given such frank criticism.

## 13 JUNE

I have just come across something copied down years ago from Hilda Vaughan's short novel *Pardon and Peace*. The speaker is Charity Evans:

'The world don't make sense of itself, sir. We're having to make our own little bit o' it, each one of us, like a patchwork quilt, I always think 't'is.'

## 14 JUNE

To the Royal Free for my massage, some shopping, then back here.

The touring production of *84 Charing Cross Road* has now come to Richmond and The Show Report for Tuesday June 12th, says, 'A great audience who gave a rousing applause at the end of Act One and Act Two. They especially liked the John Donne Complete Sermons scene. Many gave a standing ovation at the curtain.'

The cast is headed by Stefanie Powers and Clive Francis. Stefanie is brilliant at comic timing, and always the New Year's Eve scene in which Helene moans about John Donne's Complete Sermons gets a huge round of applause! This is the first time I have not directed the play, but age has caught up with me and I am relieved not to have to do it again. Whether it will come into town remains to be seen.

15 JUNE

To the optician re: new reading glasses, otherwise a quiet day.

16 JUNE

My current Blog quotes from Tony Morris' book about the Buddha:

'For the Buddha true knowledge could not be derived from second hand explanations, divine revelation, holy writ or abstract theory. It had to be grounded in direct personal experience. Clinging to views, he suggested, is dangerous, for it could easily lead to dogmatism, and from there to dispute and discord.'

Nothing is to be gained by arguing about God since no one can prove the existence of God. All we can do is speak about our inner journey, as Père Bernard Feillet has said, 'What is admirable about religions is that they are among the finest creations of human genius. They begin with the realisation that human beings, being human, know nothing of their origin, hence the evolution of myths, rituals and symbols which proclaim that within us we have more than ourselves.' Religions have evolved in an attempt to conceive the inconceivable at the heart of our experience. Which is why today faith can no longer be a matter of systematic beliefs and dogmas that claim to explain everything. When Jesus stood trial he remained silent!'

While writing the above a harsh ringing began in both my ears, a screaming sound repeated three times, a pause, then again and again. Thinking something had gone wrong with my hearing aids I pulled both out but still the screaming continued. Alarmed, I sent an SOS email to Jonathan, my doctor. How could one live with such a piercing sound, and then, suddenly I remembered that I had put some mushrooms to fry in a pan, and on entering the kitchen I found it full of smoke, which had set off the smoke alarm! I do have a habit of putting something on the stove to cook, and then get absorbed at my desk in what I am writing and so forget!

## 17 June

Reflecting further on what I wrote yesterday and what Père Bernard Feillet has written, it is clear that today hundreds of thousands have left the particular form of Christianity into which they were born. Many are exploring further afield to find other means of spiritual growth, simply because so often the churches were not nourishing their needs. Also it is not a question of following a religion but rather, as the Sufi master Inayat Khan wrote, 'It is living a religion which is necessary.'

What has to be realised is that although historically spirituality has close links with religion, it is logically prior to religion. It was Sir Alastair Hardy, the Zoologist who, in 1966, first offered a naturalistic account of religious experience when he suggested that religious awareness is a biological phenomenon that has evolved in the human species through the process of natural selection because it has a survival value. If one accepts his hypothesis then religious experience cannot be limited to members of any particular religion – in other words there must be such a thing as secular spirituality. Time and again I am moved by the sheer goodness of those who practice no religion, yet whose lives are like lanterns illuminating the surrounding darkness. Perhaps the most vivid example of such goodness is that of the fire fighters who raced into the twin towers in New York on September 11th, 2001, at risk to their own lives. I recall Mathew Parris, writing in *The Times*, commenting on how 'from time to time one meets people from whom goodness simply leaps. These people have something extraordinary. What? Could it be God? I asked myself. Is God the explanation of human goodness? ' The answer strikes him with absolute clarity,

'There is no need to explain human goodness. It exists. It can be seen and not only in the devout. Goodness is human, not divine. We do not need an outside explanation of human goodness.'

That such goodness is inherent in human nature was acknowledged by Pope John Paul ll in his Lenten message for 2003 when he said, 'the inclination to give is rooted in the depths of the human heart. Every person is conscious of a desire to interact with others and everyone finds fulfilment in a free gift of self to others.'

Spirituality, therefore, is a recognition that there is something other, something greater than the course of everyday events.

## 18 JUNE

To Amplifon in Wigmore Street where Barry Rogers increases the volume of my hearing aids for although I hear most people clearly I do have a difficulty with the lodger, who has a soft lilting voice, and one can't keep saying, 'What did you say?'

## 20 JUNE

This morning brings another glimpse of nature, this time from someone, whom I have never met, but who follows my Blog, and corresponds frequently via email. With her husband she has been creating a garden. 'This year it has really taken off, not only planting but insects, birds, squirrels, hedgehogs, slugs, snails and mice! There are advantages in not having pets! We spotted a hedgehog the other evening eating a whole blackbird by the pond in front of our little summerhouse. Perhaps the bird had broken its neck flying into a window, but we need to research hedgehog feeding skills. It took about 20 minutes and we watched from the garden room for a while, and then as it grew darker and the binoculars no longer helped, we crept out to about three feet away on the lea side and it was extraordinary to see. It ate everything, munching through all the feathers except two large ones, then wandered towards us on the grass, where it wiped its mouth and nose thoroughly like a napkin, and pottered over my feet before setting out through a shrub border and hedge to the neighbours. What a privilege!'

21 JUNE

Edward in to work in the garden.

22 JUNE

Busy packing for the trip to Rye.

## 23 June, Saturday

The lodger has picked a spray of beautiful white roses from the garden and put them in a slim vase on my desk. The gesture says everything.

Tomorrow Chris will drive the lodger and me to Rye, where we are to stay in a small cottage I have rented.

## 24 June, Sunday

Driving to Rye with the lodger and Chris in the front of the car is like being with Morecambe and Wise. One will start talking in a particular voice and the other will respond in an improvised dialogue. Or the lodger will start singing a pop song and it will then be taken up by Chris, or vice versa. I realise that I lack small talk and badinage. Too late now to change. On arrival at Wisteria Cottage, a white clap-boarded building on the side of a narrow lane which is embowered by tall trees and hedges, I go to have a pee, miss a step in the bathroom, and fall flat on my forehead, hitting the tiles. I could have cracked my skull! But I only bruise my hip. It shakes me, nonetheless, and for the next few days I am in a state of shock, and Chris buys me a walking stick.

The cottage has wisteria and sweet peas climbing up it, and by the front door there is a small patio with four wooden chairs, where we eat all our meals. It is so reminiscent of the Granary in Harpenden where Pick lived, which I have described in my memoirs.

25 JUNE

We drive to Camber Sands – the sea is far out and also too shallow for swimming, and the white sand like powder, that I daren't risk walking on it, but both Chris and the lodger go for a paddle. The gulls wheel threateningly over the many groups picnicking on the sands. In the evening we watch on television a film, *Mystic River*, but the Bostonian accents are so thick that I don't understand a word.

26 JUNE

The shock of the fall has made me very unsteady on my feet. We drive to see the garden at Great Dixter, and in the evening watch the film *Calvary*, but the thick Irish accents mean I don't understand this either!

27 JUNE

We drive into Rye, meet up with Norman, in what was once a monastery but is now a gallery for large-scale antiques such as a circular table fourteen feet in width. Everything is on that scale, costing thousands of pounds. The owner travels the world visiting old castles, collecting antiques for the very wealthy and those who have large rooms.

## 28 JUNE

We drive to Sissinghurst, superior in so many ways to Great Dixter, the gardens – a series of rooms, are much better tended, but then the National Trust can afford more gardeners. Also the buildings are very superior. In the evening Chris puts on the film, *Shawshank Redemption*, and while again I cannot decipher the American accents I am moved by the sheer quality of the acting, especially that of Morgan Freeman.

## 29 JUNE

We drive back to London, loaded with plants from Great Dixter and from Sissinghurst.

## 30 JUNE

Saturday and Sunday I am still badly shaken by my fall, and the lodger is concerned that I may be dehydrated so he buys medicines for me and insists I call for a house visit from a doctor. One comes but can't find much wrong with me, and I am convinced it is the effects of the shock.

# JULY 2018

## 1 JULY

Today, being the first Sunday in the month, our meditation group meets and it is my turn to speak.

## 2 JULY, MONDAY

The heat is overwhelming. I try and rest, as well as drink a lot of liquids.

## 4 JULY, WEDNESDAY

I have my hair cut but have acute gout in my right hand so I cannot put any weight on it, or use it at all.

## 5 July, Thursday

Jonathan rings with a prescription for the gout and I realise it is the result of my drinking red wine – I ought to remember by now!

## 6 July, Friday

The pain has now gone. But the heat is too much for me. I go to the Eye Place to be tested for new reading glasses, then back to start cooking food for the lunch on Sunday.

## 7 July, Saturday

Too hot to write. Anne comes to give me an Alexander lesson, and I spend much time in the kitchen preparing lunch for tomorrow, a day that would have marked another birthday for Hywel, but which was also the day on which he died. On Monday is the big launch of *A Life Shared* at Daunt's in Marylebone High Street, about 60 people expected.

## 8 July, Sunday

A day of continuing intense heat. Norman, Carl and Jonathan arrive, and with the lodger we sit in the garden, drinking champagne. But where is Richard

Wilson? In the end I telephone him and he says 'Oh is it today? Right I'll come now!' It is a lively lunch and at one point Richard raises his glass and we all drink to the memory of Hywel who would have been 82 today! The lodger was such a help and made it all easier.

I learn the words of my speech tomorrow.

9 JULY, MONDAY

The evening is a great success. Stefanie Powers looking ravishingly young and beautiful, just off to Kenya, embraces me with such warmth. Clive Francis also there and Rosie Thomas. I gather there is a serious chance of 84 going to New York. Maureen Lipman, Rula Lenska, Isabelle Amyes, Jessica Barnes, Dan, Donald Howarth, Peter Eyre, Virginia Ironside, Ruth Pavey, and many more. Tony Morris and I go up to the long balcony at Daunt's in Marylebone – a bit like the Pope appearing on the balcony at St Peter's, especially as I am all in white. Tony makes a splendid speech and I follow. After thanking various people I went on to say,

'This story begins on one Saturday night in 1958, when at the age of 31 I, never having been in a gay pub, went in a fit of loneliness to our local gay pub in Hampstead, the William the 4th. The same evening Hywel Jones, aged 22, newly arrived in London, also never having been to a gay pub, paid a visit to the William the 4th. But for that coincidence we may never have met.

Of course, we were then, like countless others, criminals in the eyes of the law, and also there were few role models for two men wanting to share their lives, so like others, we had to make up the rules as we went along.

Hywel had a mischievous sense of humour, which belied his deeper seriousness. The impresario Michael Codron, for whom Hywel played the young Laurie Lee in *Cider with Rosie*, always used to call him Pixie. When he first arrived in London he went to work as telephonist at a block of flats run by his cousin Edie, in return for a room. All went well until the day when the phone rang and Hywel, in his most mischievous mood, picked it up, saying 'Buckingham Palace here. I am afraid that Her Majesty is out cleaning windows.' The caller was not amused. She was the owner of the flats. So that job was taken from him and he was put to hoovering carpets. Indeed, all went well for that job too until the day he enjoyed a prolonged coffee break and left the hoover running and, on his return, found it had burned a hole in the carpet!

He loved telling stories and often when I was in the kitchen preparing food I would hear gales of laughter coming from the dining room where Hywel would be entertaining our guests. One of his favourite stories had been told to him by Helen Higham, the wife of the distinguished literary agent, David Higham.

Helen used to come to Hywel weekly for lessons in the Alexander technique, of which he was a very gifted exponent. Once a year David Higham would hold a soirée in his large Hampstead house for some of his distinguished clients, one of whom was Edith Sitwell. On this particular occasion at five o'clock the front door bell rang and little Mathew Higham, aged nine, ran to the door. It was Dame Edith's chauffeur come to collect her. Mathew ran back into the main room where Dame Edith was holding court, and said at the top of his voice, 'Dame Edith, you've got to go now!' She drew herself and, looking at Mathew, said, 'Mathew, the next time I have a soirée you must come to it. There will be, for sure, a number of people I shall want you to say that to!'

Thank you all for coming, may you enjoy the book and spread the word!'

In the course of the evening Maureen Lipman reminds me of a valuable note I once gave her after seeing a one-woman show she had put together. I told her that it was relentless, never for one moment was she silent... and I recalled the magic moment when Marlene Dietrich gave her one-woman show in the West End. Towards the end she stood quietly humming to herself, with the orchestra playing behind her softly. It was as though the last of her guests had gone, and we were now alone with her. It was unforgettable. 'That' said Maureen, 'was the most valuable note!'

I was also reminded of a sudden speech in Macbeth as played by Robert Eddison. In the speech, on hearing of his wife's death, he says, 'Tomorrow and tomorrow and tomorrow creeps in this petty pace from day to day', and he went through at a great speed to 'It is a tale told by an idiot, full of sound and fury signifying...' and then he stopped. It was electrifying, the sudden chasm of silence into which he appeared to be looking, this sense of desolation, before saying the final word 'nothing!'

The great pianist Clifford Curzon claimed that a performer's whole art could be detected in 'the space between the notes.' Debussy also said, 'Music is the space between the notes' while another great pianist, who had taught Curzon, Artur Schnabel commented, 'The notes I handle no better than other pianists. But the pauses between the notes. Ah, that is where the real art resides!'

It was the same with Gielgud when I directed him in Hugh Whitemore's *The Best of Friends*. At the very end of the play Sir Sydney Cockerell says, 'The angel of Death seems to have quite passed me by.' He then paused, and added with a twinkle, 'Who knows, I may pop off tonight!' And the curtain slowly fell.

It is, of course, the art of rhetoric of which Churchill was perhaps the last exponent in English politics. I recall Esmé Percy, who had been trained as an actor by Sarah Bernhardt, and became a superb exponent of Shaw's plays, telling me how to deal with the long speeches in Don Juan in Hell. 'The thing is,' he said, 'to build a speech to a climax and then pause on a preposition such as 'but – if – or' and then start to build the following speech to the next proposition.' A brilliant note.

## 10 July

To the Royal Free for an x-ray of my thyroid, then back for a quiet day!

## 11 July

Peter de B comes to coffee and a long chat. He would like to rent a disused church and live in it and maintain the graveyard, so I have emailed Rowan Williams to ask if there is an organisation for redundant churches that he can approach.

## 12 July

In the morning to the Royal Free to be fitted with a 24-hour ECG meter. In the afternoon to the Macmillan Cancer Centre to see a thyroid specialist. He puts a tiny camera through my nose and down my throat, and says all is well, but he would like me in August to have an MRI scan of the underside of my tongue.

## 13 July

Edward comes to the garden. I return the monitor to the Royal Free. In the afternoon Carl Miller comes to sort out problems with my new computer. He has enormous patience. I prepare nibbles for Mair, Hywel's sister, and her husband Walter, who are coming for drinks in the garden at 6 p.m. Walter sees a copy of the sayings of Lao-Tzu and asks to look at it. He is so taken with it that I suggest he borrow it.

15 July

Even now in old age I rejoice that I am still learning – and also unlearning! One has to shed if one is to put forth new growth. There is a pattern and a purpose that makes each life unique: this is what is meant by following one's destiny. In the quiet practice of meditation we perceive new possibilities.

There was a period in my life when I was working non-stop, with two productions in the West End, a tour, a weekly column to write, books to review, teaching, and running the Bleddfa Centre. I was drained and exhausted! It was then that my partner quietly said, 'the answer is in yourself.' I had stopped meditating! And so returning to the practice brought new energy and above all, new growth.'

16 July

Too hot!

17 July

Flowers arrive from Allan Walter, the colours of a peacock's wings.

20 July

To the Royal Free where Roby Rakhit tells me my heart is in good condition now that they have got the medication right. He also suggested I take only two Dixogin a day, and reduce the Levothyroxine dose.

21 July

Off early for an MRI scan at the Macmillan Cancer Centre on my throat. I am strapped tightly in then glided inside, and for 45 minutes have to endure loud pop music! The occasional thumps from the machine sound like an ogre trying to knock down the house! Back to give lunch in the garden to Penny Wesson, my long time agent and friend, and Gill Treuthardt, who did so much to sort out Hywel's and my financial affairs. I retire early, exhausted, while the lodger kindly does the washing up.

## 22 July

The intense heat continues, but I make three jars of Tomato Chutney, à la Theodora Fitzgibbon's recipe.

The lodger does all our laundry and each day I clean the top of the stove, with its crumbs and food stains, and wipe down the marble, and rinse all the dishes that have food on, as this helps to keep down the number of fruit flies with which we have been pestered this summer! I swat them as they appear on the white marble tiles of the bathroom, an easy target – when will they learn. What with foxes at large, straying cats, squirrels, and endless snails, one is battling daily! One reads of raucous gulls swooping onto baby's prams, and recently a fox got in through an open window and bit the cheek of a woman sleeping in bed!

## 23 July

The temperature is even higher and will be so for the rest of the week!

## 24 July

It is like living in an oven. All I want to do is lie on my bed and wait for this heatwave to pass, but suppose it doesn't? Clearly the whole climate is changing, not just politically. Is this perhaps Yeats' Beast hurtling towards

Bethlehem to be born, when, as he writes, 'the centre falls apart'?

25 JULY

The lodger is away for two days to attend his brother's wedding. Because it is even hotter today he says that on no account must I go out, and he buys in food and water for me for the next two days so that I don't have to sally forth. I am moved by his concern for me.

26 JULY

The heat is even more oppressive today.

27 JULY

I am in such pain in my right shoulder that Tusse comes to massage it for me. She was here last night to talk about certain personal problems and we sat in the garden drinking prosecco. She brought a salad of pear, Roquefort cheese and endive which the lodger and I will share this evening with the roast chicken I bought from M&S. If Chris comes we shall share it with him.

## 28 July

Sipping coffee, I recall Virginia Woolf's description of Hardy after a visit to him in Dorchester as 'of one delivered of all his work.' And I reflect that, apart from this current book, it is the same for me. It has been a full and rich life, exploring, and above all constantly learning so that, when the moment comes, I shall be ready to slip away quietly. I have no fear of dying, it is simply the final chapter in this volume of existence. As in John Donne's famous description:

'All mankind is one volume. When one man dies one chapter is torn out of the book and translated into a better language, and every chapter must be so translated. God employs several translators: some pieces are translated by age, some by sickness, some by war, some by justice. But God's hand shall bind up all our scattered leaves again for that library where every book shall be open to another.'

## 29 July

Given the statistics for the higher rate of divorce today I am reminded that the fall-out is often caused by differences of personality with neither partner willing to be flexible. Yet the art of any successful relationship lies in acknowledging and accepting such differences.

## 30 July

Strange how memories suddenly rise to the surface. This time of the actress Liz Fraser who was in many of the *Carry On* films and whom I was directing in a tour of Michael Frayn's comedy, *Donkeys' Years*. She used to work for the Samaritans. She was about to do a new play and it was her last evening when a woman rang to say that her husband, who went off each Monday to work away, returning home on Friday, was having an affair with a nudist. What should she do? 'It is a strict rule of the Samaritans', said Liz, 'that you never use humour, but for some reason on this occasion I heard myself saying, "When your husband returns this Friday answer the door wearing no clothes!" Liz then started rehearsals but was rung by the Samaritans to say the woman had been ringing a week later saying 'What do I do now?' Liz was fired from the Samaritans in consequence!

This morning I took a mini-cab to Gay's the Word bookshop with a pile of copies of *A Life Shared* and sat with Jimmy McSweeney, the manager, in his tiny office. We talked about his brother Gerald in Cork, who was a great friend of mine when I lived there and whom I recall one evening, seated in my house, somewhere around 11 in the evening, when a harsh loud ringing come from his pocket. Out came an old-fashioned alarm clock that he switched off with a grin, saying, '11 30 in the evening is when I was born!'

He was someone I felt I had always known and often at Ballywilliam we would sit of an evening on the upper terrace, swathed in blankets, watching the sunset. We seemed never to run out of things to talk about. He was so appreciative of everything. Quietness flowed around him. His conversation was constantly full of surprises like his own garden with its narrow terraces and zigzagging paths, leading from one bower to the next, with ever widening views of the estuary as one climbed; finding small statues in the undergrowth, or a sign from a church saying 'Kneel and pray', or a bench inviting one to sit and appreciate the view, until one reached the top most level, above the roof of his house, where he had created an eight-sided belvedere.

He told me of a character, Adrienne, now very old, who came into his second-hand bookshop in Cork and barked at him, 'I suppose you know Dick is dead!'

'Yes.'

'You didn't come to the funeral!'

'No.'

'Hm! Cost too much money I suppose?'

'No, I thought if I came you would think I was after his books!'

'Jolly right too! What about lunch tomorrow? I've sold his gold fillings. At least he was good for something!'

And then there was another story of how he was once a guest at Adrienne's for lunch when two lady friends got lost and were late arriving. When finally they appeared, she just said, 'You're late! Pee that way, eat this way!' And after coffee had been served she picked up the tray, saying, 'Well, you can go now!'

31 JULY

Ireland is so rich in its characters that it is not surprising it continues to produce so many writers – the material is at hand! Being friends of Molly Keane, we met many, including her friend Hurd Hatfield, the American actor, who had long made his home in Ireland. He was perhaps famous for one role, that of the title role in the American movie of Oscar Wilde's *The Portrait of Dorian Gray*. Each summer his great friend Maggie Williams would come over from the States to visit him. Having met him with Molly, Hywel and I were invited to dinner. We stumbled through the overgrown bushes to the front door and knocked. Suddenly Hurd opened the door and we were ushered into a spacious hall with a white stone floor lit by candlelight.

Maggie, emerging from a candlelit drawing room, tall and elegant in a long woollen knitted dress, extended a ringed hand to us to. The whole place was like a film set with fires burning in every room, or so it seemed at first, until we realised that there was just crushed newspaper in every fireplace to which Hurd, going ahead, applied a match, so that as we entered each room a fire was flickering! He took us on a tour of the downstairs rooms while Maggie photographed us for the archives. Then Hurd disappeared down a dark and unlit corridor to prepare the next scene for us. When we entered the kitchen where we were to dine, he had deliberately under lit it so that it was like stepping into a painting by Rembrandt. One could just glimpse beams overhead, and pots of geraniums in the shuttered window embrasures, while on the far side was an enormous fireplace where a single log burned. As in a Dutch painting the candlelight focused on the foreground: a table set with fine china, a bowl of pink roses, and a large white china stand containing a mauve cabbage and a white cauliflower as decoration. The conversation was gentle, humorous, anecdotal, with both Hurd and Maggie acting as perfect hosts. I played my supporting role, able to appreciate many of his references, knowing the people, such as Tennessee Williams and others, about whom he spoke.

After dinner he took us on a tour upstairs where all his past was laid out, framed in glass cabinets, while on the walls were posters of the various plays and films in which he had appeared, together with photographs of him with this celebrity and that. We were taken into his bathroom, which resembled a Victorian actor's dressing room. On top of the bath were wooden shutters and placed at one end a heavy prop crown that he had worn in some production. The landing resembled a Gentleman's Club such as the Garrick, with portraits of Henry Irving, Tennessee Williams and others. The entire house was partly a stage set and partly a heritage walk through Hurd's minuscule career, from Michael Chekhov who was his teacher and whom he revered, to Dorian Gray, Lord Byron (a part which he doubled with that of Don Quixote in the original Broadway production of Tennessee William's *Camino Real*), and to recent photographs of his one-man play about Whistler, written for him by Maggie, and which he had just performed in Russia, in Stanislavsky's own house!

He described how he and Maggie appeared in London at the first night of Neil Bartlett's adaptation and production of *Dorian Gray* at the Lyric Theatre, Hammersmith, and when they entered the auditorium, like visiting royalty, the whole audience was rising to its feet. Maggie hissed to Hurd, 'It's not us you fool, it's the Queen!'

Hurd was like a Prospero with his effects, having created a museum of his own ego. And yet able to poke fun at himself, as when he was last in London and telephoned John Gielgud.

'I telephoned John and when I said "it's Hurd", he replied, "Oh no!" and rang off!'

There was such a touching vulnerability and charm alongside his ego-centredness. Was it, I wondered, a substitute for a career that never really got anywhere because he was more a handsome face than a fine actor?

There was something very Edward Albee about him. In the past he would take visitors up to the bedroom and, opening a large wardrobe, show them dresses his mother wore to each of his premieres.

# AUGUST 2018

## 1 August

Last night I made some more apple chutney, as per the Theodora Fitzgibbon recipe, but badly burned the bottom of the lodger's large saucepan – I had added, as she suggests, some cornflour to thicken it, but while it is said a watched pot never boils, in this case an unwatched pot burned. I scrubbed and scrubbed but only got half of the black removed so I left a note saying, 'Me culpa, and I will buy a new saucepan' but the lodger said, no problem, I will clean it, and he did! Relief all round the domestic front.

It is evening and I was having a whiskey and dolce cheese on Melba toast when I dropped one by the desk, exclaiming 'Oh, fuck, bloody hell!' I find I am frequently dropping things and this must be related to old age. So for all my years of meditation I am still capable of such explosions. But all over within a minute.

2 August

Little to report. I struggle to fill in forms for Advanced Medical Treatment – forms cause me to freeze with fright. The lodger tells me I have filled it in incorrectly, so I have to start all over again. The heat continues.

3 August

Letter from Peter Dukes arrives. His mother Mania was one of the team of voluntary helpers in the early years of the Hampstead Theatre when, without grants, we lurched from one financial crisis to another. The Friends of Hampstead Theatre, as they were known, acted as volunteer programme sellers, helpers in the box office, and stuffing envelopes each month, while Mania Dukes managed the coffee bar. Peter eventually graduated in law and must now be in his 70s. He has published a book, all about God, the divine, and spirituality; a copy of which I have ordered entitled *The Fallacy of the Excluded Alternative*. But what most enchants me in his letter is the following: 'I think I once told you that when I was about 10 or 11 years old I had a pet pigeon. He was called Jimmie. The day before yesterday a beautiful white dove with black wings and a deep blue-purple and greenish neck alighted on my roof terrace, sidled up to my chair and stayed. I was engrossed in your spiritual writings. So Jimmie had returned!

He then followed me indoors, hopping into my living room and staying the night, prior to flying off the next day. So, goodbye Jimmie. Thanks for the visit.

Yesterday afternoon, however, he was back again, happily sitting on my arm, and again stayed the night. And there he is still today. So, good morning Jimmie.'

I go for my weekly massage with Keith Hunt. He is just back from a week in Disneyland, taking his wife, two daughters, and their three children. I said 'at this rate you can't afford to retire!'

## 4 AUGUST

Although I am very patient with people, I do find repeatedly in old age that I am often impatient with things. Once again, last night, getting entangled in my sheet, I said, 'What's the matter with you? Why are you so recalcitrant?' Where did that word come from? It is not one I ever recall using.

## 5 AUGUST, SUNDAY

Our meditation day when Ruth will be giving a short talk. I receive an email from a friend who has ceased meditating because, she says, she's afraid of finding nothing there. I reflect on this, and then reply that perhaps the mistake is to be expecting something or someone (God?) to manifest itself.

The Buddha's teaching of mindfulness is quite simply to listen to the silence, gently disengaging from passing thoughts and emotions. Just being. Easier said than done, of course. But if one perseveres, it is the silence that so enriches one.

I have just come across an entry in my Ballywilliam journal, describing a day in our Irish home when it rained all night, wind roaring in the chimney, racing around the house, vibrating the bushes and shrubs, while a mist blanked out the grey sea. I looked at Peter Eugene Ball's sculpture of St Patrick that stood on the pine cupboard in my studio. A staff in one hand, and two cowbells in the other, leaning forward slightly, the deep indentation of his eyes made it seem as though he was gauging the storm, and I reflected. Sometimes one has to set out, staff in hand, ringing one's pilgrim bell, going through the mist and mystery, enduring the storm; while at other times one must wait for the storm to abate before setting out on one's journey.

How curious my life, so rich, with so many strands, but what have I achieved? Is achievement the sole goal? For myself it is not in the plays I have directed, the books I have written, nor in founding the Hampstead Theatre and the Bleddfa Trust, but in the richness of my life in general and, above all, the strength of my relationship with Hywel. When, at one literary event for the launch of my memoirs someone asked, 'Mr Roose-Evans, of your many achievements which do you value most?' My immediate reply was my (then) 52-year relationship with Hywel Jones.This reply brought loud applause from the audience. Love and friendship have been the central force in my life.

## 6 August

I reflect often on two brush ink drawings that hang in my bedroom, given to me by a Chinese artist in America. One is of a Buddhist monk, setting off, staff in hand, through a dense fog, a cloud of unknowing. The other is of a monk, seated cross-legged in meditation on the edge of a cliff, gazing into the void below which is swirling with mist and mystery. There is time to journey and a time to be still.

## 7 August

Daunt's have asked for more copies of *A Life Shared* and I take these in, also buying John Boyne's latest novel. But at the moment I'm deeply engrossed in Phillip Pullman's new book, which is un-put-downable, he is such a masterly storyteller.

## 8 August

The weather much cooler. I finish the Pullman and am launched on a frightening novel, recommended by the lodger, entitled *Tony and Susan* by Austin Wright. It is truly scary!

## 9 August

Every now and then one wakes up with an entire dream in one's consciousness, every detail, and when that happens it is important to write it down. Such dreams carry important messages. I have had several in my life but one more recent one was so powerful that on waking I immediately closed my eyes in order to go back into it, absorbing its atmosphere of silence and stillness.

In the dream I am walking with the actress Jane Lapotaire down the main street of a small country town. The impression is that we have come from a place of deep silence. It is very early in the morning. There is no one else about. It is all very still and hushed. We come to a corner where I observe what was once a 12th century Catholic Church but now a Quaker Meeting House. On the door is a circular handle carved in wood, the shape of a flower. I intimate to Jane (no words are spoken) that we should enter the Meeting House for worship, but Jane intimates that we should go on, that we should stay in the open.

At the end of the street, on the opposite side, I see an arch leading to an Oxford College and my thought is that I would like to show Jane this ancient place of learning. But now she is leaning with her head against a wall, listening intently to the silence. I realise I am meant to do the same. There is such a freshness in the air, presaging a day of great heat. The silence is so intense and the air so pure.

That was the dream and I had much to learn from it but I was especially intrigued by the detail of the place of learning, and Jane Lapotaire (the anima in Jungian psychology, or Sophia, the figure of wisdom) saying no, simply listen.

The lesson of absolute silence has yet to be learned by churches and synagogues, and indeed in mosques. I am reminded how in Buddhist monasteries the abbot will give to individual monks what is called a koan. A koan is a spiritual riddle. It does not make intellectual sense, but once it has been cracked the individual takes a leap forwards into a deeper and more intuitive understanding of the nature of reality, of the ultimate oneness of all creation. And so I end with one of the most famous koans:

What is the sound of one hand clapping? And the answer that came to me was: Silence!

As Rumi wrote, 'Stay in the root of your being: don't climb out on intellectual branches!'

## 10 August

To Stavros to have my hair cut, then to get a copy of Peter Conradi's review of *Blue Remembered Hills* in *The Radnorshire Transactions*. He heads the article 'Magus and Shaman'. I tell him I am neither of these; I might be called a Showman, and Magician, as I do occasionally pull a rabbit out of a hat.

More rain and plants that were flattened by the heat and barely responded to my daily watering are now standing upright.

## 11 August

John Rowlands-Pritchard has sent me a copy of Paul Robertson's book, *Soundscapes: A Musician's Journey through Life and Death*. A renowned musician and leader of the Medici Quartet, he nearly died as a result of a ruptured aorta. During the long period of unconsciousness he had a profound Near Death Experience, of which he says, 'in common with many others who survive NDE, I am now absolutely intent on living without adding any further lies or unfinished business to my existence. Such accumulated deceit, especially self-deceit, proves a cruelly heavy burden when the call comes to travel lightly, as it must.'

Elsewhere he says, 'Silence, the ultimate spiritual journey... at the end of everything lies silence – the ultimate paradox, and its deeper resolution. The lesson of absolute silence is ever deeper and increasingly richly imbued with meaning, making it all the more engrossing and beautiful. At this level beauty lies beyond definition – closer perhaps to the pure union of love or perfection.'

And I think of the quietness that Hywel and I shared in those last two weeks of his life when he could neither move nor speak. I felt no need to speak, simply to gaze into each other's eyes.

Robertson also had this observation that this kind of silence explains why, in a therapeutic relationship, some people are able to listen quite differently from others and thereby change the emotional space between them.

12 AUGUST, SUNDAY

Rupert comes to breakfast after Mass at St Dominic's. He lies stretched out on the sofa, talking about his life. All I have to do is listen. When he goes, after clearing the table and resetting it for lunch, I have a lie down while the lodger prepares the food.

14 AUGUST

Another quote from Paul Robertson:

'My experience as I died was that I had no wish to carry anything with me and was gladly able to shed

my superficial ego and individual personality in
order to travel beyond the threshold of myself into
the transcendent, eternal beauty of the universe.
At this precious moment the longing to join this
Infinity was so powerful that I suddenly saw all my
familiar psychological apparel merely as an old suit
of clothes that could be gladly abandoned.

But if the next life is so appealing, why do we cling so
desperately to this earthly existence? And if the sight of
eternity is as glorious as I suggest, why would anyone
want to return? These seem entirely natural questions
which I continue to ask myself.'

15 AUGUST

An actor friend of mine who is now off to Northern
Ireland to play Pozzo in Waiting for Godot, part of the
annual Beckett Festival on top of a mountain, asks if
he can read it aloud, with me reading the other characters. He often drops by when he has an audition and
I read in the other characters, and we do this several
times.

16 AUGUST

Sharon arrives to clean and says, 'Why is your fridge
hot on the outside?' It was second-hand so maybe it is

coming to an end. I go for my weekly massage with Keith Hunt and ask him about the fridge. He at once says – 'Switch it off!' Apparently this is how the fire started at Grenfell Tower. I hasten back and switch it off and remove all the content – I might have set the whole house on fire.

This afternoon to the Macmillan Cancer Centre for another x-ray, Francis Vaz says that the recent scan shows nothing alarming, that all is clear, and that the slight uncomfortable feeling I have when swallowing is due simply to age. I return greatly relieved.

17 August

There is much dialogue and discussion at present within the Catholic Church re: shared communion where a married couple one of whom may be Catholic and the other not, and the latter is denied Communion. I think at once of two stories told to me by a Catholic nun, sister Marcella, who has worked for many years for L'Arche. One story is about the annual pilgrimage to Canterbury and of the occasion when one of the group was Robert, who had Downs Syndrome, who was also a Catholic. On arrival they all attended a Eucharist celebrated by Robert Runcie, then Archbishop. Robert insisted on going up for Communion and, as the Archbishop came to him, he looked up and said, 'What's your name?' The Archbishop replied 'Robert' whereupon the other, reaching out his hand said 'I'm Robert too!' and they both shook hands. When Robert Runcie gave him the Host he broke it into two and handed half back to the Archbishop.

The other story is of an occasion in one of the L'Arche houses, a weekly Catholic Mass was being celebrated. One of those present, a woman who was Anglican, said at the moment of communion, 'Just a crumb, Father! Just a crumb!'

## 18 AUGUST

Diana Walker, one of the first trustees of the Belddfa Trust, has just sent me the brochure of the 1987 Festival of the Tree at Bleddfa. On the final page I quote the words of Dame Meinrad Craighead OSB at Stanbrook Abbey: 'Let me look up upwards into the branches of the towering oak to know that it grew great and strong because it grew slowly and well. Slow me down, O Lord, and inspire me to send my roots deeper into the soil of life's enduring values that I may grow towards the stars of my future destiny.'

That is all we can do – put down our roots into deeper soil, allowing our branches to reach up and outwards.

9 p.m. I have just been in the kitchen to open a packet of Melba toast, and they fell out on the floor, breaking into smaller pieces. 'Fuck the bloody things!' I scream.

I have yet to get used to and accept that, philosophically, this is simply a symptom of old age.

20 AUGUST

I listen to a number of Beethoven recordings, especially Quartet 130, in which the Cavatina is so haunting, a yearning and a letting go, incredibly sad, followed by the final, joyful Allegro movement.

21 AUGUST

Sorting out papers I find a notebook in which I have recorded a number of anecdotes. Here is one, a host saying to a guest, 'Well, I hope you enjoyed yourself?' to which the guest responded, 'Well I certainly haven't enjoyed anyone else!' And one more from this store of stories, it is set in Ireland. The foreman of a building site interviewing a builder, said, 'I have to ask you two questions. What is a girder and what is a joist?'

The chap replies, 'Oh, I know that! Goethe wrote Faust and Joyce wrote Ulysses!'

22 AUGUST

To the Donmar to see *The Aristocrats*, but I have difficulty understanding the accents.

## 23 AUGUST

To Gay's the Word in the morning to deliver more copies of *A Life Shared*. I buy the TLS and read Libby Purves' moving review of the book. In the afternoon Lucy Letherbridge comes to interview me for a profile in *The Tablet*.

## 24 AUGUST

To the Royal Free for my massage.

## 25 AUGUST

Anne comes to give my Alexander lesson, bringing a pot of Sweet Cecily.

In the evening Norman and Chris come to supper, a lively sharing, almost like a family.

## 26 AUGUST

Thinking of birthdays I recalled how when the scholar and writer, Dame Felicitas Corrigan, OSB of Stanbrook Abbey, was about to be 80, Dame Philippa Edwards asked me if I could think of a special way of marking the occasion. I consulted Hugh Whitemore and our producer Michael Redington and they suggested balloons! Philippa recalls, 'that marvellous surprise for Dame Felicitas' birthday by the arrival of a man bearing 80 helium balloons. 40 were held in each of the deliveryman's hands. I was near the enclosure door when he arrived as arranged and managed to bring Dame Felicitas along quickly to receive them. She was quite overwhelmed. You and I had planned that we would release them into the air in a great silver cloud but, in fact, and fortunately, lots of people held onto them and attached at least one to Dame F's chair in the refectory and tethered them in various other places so that we had them for several days until the last bit of helium had leaked from the last one. It was a happy pandemonium in the cloister, which is usually a place of absolute silence! A delightful memory.'

## 27 August

As Lao Tzu wrote, 'Less and less effort is used until things resolve themselves.' One of the important aspects of ageing is learning to let go!

## 28 August

To the surgery for my warfarin test, and a shop at M&S, but I get the wrong bus (46) instead of the C11 and am carried all the way up to Hampstead before I realised! I got out and decided to walk home, pulling the trolley, which contained four bottles of prosecco plus other items.

## 29 AUGUST

Am fighting a head cold. The lodger gives me kaloba pelargonium cough and cold tablets. I find it difficult to meditate. I must just be patient!

## 30 AUGUST

I struggle all day with this head cold, the nose streaming, the throat sore, and so just after six I retire to bed. Around nine, on his return, the lodger knocks on the door and says would I like some pasta in sauce. So I put on my dressing gown and sit in the centre room with him, enjoying this comforting surprise.

At night, whenever I am awake, I repeat my mantra, as I do during the day. As I lie there in the dark I have an ever-deepening sense of being held and surrounded by love, which has grown over the years. Yet it is a puzzle to me how many do not have this experience, how concepts such as God get in the way.

## 31 AUGUST

The lodger urges me to stay in bed, which I shall do. I get up at one o'clock and dress but am groggy on my feet so I shall not attempt to go out.

I have discovered in this old notebook, entitled *Antics and Oddities*, the following two stories which I have passed on to Keith Hunt at the Royal Free to add to his repertoire.

The first is about a man whose mother-in-law went to Denver, Colorado for her health and there died. A telegram was sent to the son-in-law: 'Mother-in-law dead. Shall we embalm, cremate or bury?' The answer came: 'Embalm, cremate and bury. Take no risks!'

The other story is of an old lady who died in Russia and her nephew, after ascertaining that her will was satisfactory, called to have the body embalmed and sent to England for burial. In due course the coffin arrived but when it was unscrewed they were dismayed to find it contained the remains not of the aunt but of a Russian general who had died and been embalmed at the same time. They telegraphed to Russia to ask that the mistake be rectified, and got back the answer: 'Your aunt buried with full military honours: do what you please with the General!'

That's enough for today – I am now going back to bed.

# SEPTEMBER 2018

1 SEPTEMBER

The lodger urges me to stay in bed.

2 SEPTEMBER

This week's *The Tablet* is full of the news of the Pope's visit to Ireland. He is a man of great humility and compassion but I am puzzled that he calls upon the whole Church to atone for the world wide sex scandals committed by clergy and religious – surely it is only the latter who should do penance? For too long these scandals were hushed up in order to protect the name of the Church, but Jesus never came to found a Church!

What, I often think, do the poor in Rome think of the hundreds of yards of expensive material that go into the making of the robes of Cardinals! Indeed,

*The Tablet* reported earlier that there is one Cardinal in Rome who has, in the hall of his apartment, on a pedestal under a glass dome his Cardinal's hat, and that on entering his apartment, visitors are expected to kneel and kiss his signet ring. Unlike Pope Francis, who simply shakes hands with people.

So where does the future lie? I recall Cardinal Nicholls suggesting that it lay in small groups meeting in one another's homes, studying the scriptures, and other writings, sitting in silent meditation, and then perhaps breaking some bread and drinking wine – it doesn't need a priest to do this. Father Richard Rohr, a Franciscan who founded the Centre for Contemplation in the desert at Albuquerque has said that his prayer for the Church is that it should grow less rich, less powerful, more concerned as was Jesus with 'two or three gathered together in my name,' rather than in vast numbers.

3 SEPTEMBER

People are endlessly fascinating, which is why there will always be novelists and dramatists who open windows into the lives of others, so that in reading or listening, we become a little wiser.

How richly different are people's lives. There are some homes you walk into and there is such a sense of calm and order, and you realise that it is a home created out of love. Manley Hopkins touches on this in his poem 'The Vale of Elwy'. And then there are other homes where a great deal of money has been spent on the latest interior design, with many hard surfaces, and enormous sofas, more like settings for cocktail parties than a home. Each room, each house, each flat to some extent reflects the person living there, but only part, you can't judge a person solely by the state of their home! But the most comfortable are those that have a feeling of really having been lived in.

## 4 September

I sleep late, and then go to collect medicines from Boots. I am still dizzy and uncertain on my feet so I am glad I have cancelled all engagements for this week. The lodger brings me a dish of carrot sticks and humus mixed with oil and strong pepper. Delicious!

## 5 September

Elizabeth Halls writes from Wales to tell me of her aunt who would spend many hours on end, with the cat on her knee, in meditative silence, prayer, and contemplation, seated by her Aga.

'She did so much practically for others in our little village community and was such fun, beloved by many. In the last months before her death from cancer, she didn't want to go to chapel, or to have the people from the chapel come to pray with her, but they and every-one else were welcome to come and just be with her. Often they would read a book or chat but often they would just sit with her in a complete and un-accustomed but beautiful silence in front of the fire. They still talk about it.'

I find myself very moved by this, especially as in old age I have felt less and less the need to go to church. For me there are too many words, and all too often little sense of the sacred, whereas in our meditation group the silence is so powerful. Which is why, as I have mentioned before, the future lies, I think, in small groups meeting in one another's homes. Our society has less and less sense of being part of a community which is why we are going to need these small cells of activities more and more.

I spend the afternoon sorting out my bills, invoices, bank statements, etc. and placing them into different envelopes, ready for Nick Beardwood, my accountant.

The lodger has an unexpected free evening so he lies on the sofa reading as I sit in my armchair, and I find his prolonged presence and sharing of the space very healing.

Now at 10 p.m. to bed as the cold is moving down to my chest. The lodger makes me a drink of hot rum with lemon and cloves and I fall asleep in the arms of Morpheus, the god of dreams. How interesting that in his name is that of another god – Orpheus, the god of music – so I am sleeping between two gods.

## 6 September

Elizabeth Halls, who works as a counsellor in the Ludlow and Leominster area, and who wrote to me about her aunt, also adds these reflections on old age:

'Often we think of old age, and as it is commonly portrayed, as a dwindling and a losing; and so it is, the good Lord knows, but that is not the whole story. Sometimes someone shows us differently, lives it differently, dies it differently; and those of us who work with the dying sometimes see, through them, that there is a 'through' and 'beyond' that leads us all ever forward. The pattern of death and resurrection is written into us, into life, into the universe.'

My cold has now descended to my chest, but the sun shines and I have just ordered some attar of roses as the lodger says that the petals make delicious tea!

## 7 September

I still can't shake off this cold so decided to stay in bed all morning. Now up for a simple lunch and this entry before returning to bed.

What I have learned in old age is that love has so many facets, and platonic love is one aspect. And I think back to my friendship with Ethel Spencer-Pickering when I was in my early twenties and she in her eighties, and there was a deep love between us. Once,

when she had her stroke and for some time was immo-
bilised in her four-poster bed, I went into her room to
say goodnight and kissed her gently on the lips for the
first, and only, time. She responded so warmly, and
with a shiver, that I realised it was many a long year
since she had been kissed and I began also to suspect
that her marriage to Spencer Pickering was probably
not even consummated.

Years later, I discovered something she wrote to her
niece when I went off for a year to teach in New York:

'Then one day Jimmie went to work in America and
I thought that I should never see him again. It was
autumn. I remember going to the door and giving him
a last embrace, then dropping my arms, letting him go,
as one does a wild bird – for I never hoped to possess
him. How can the old contain the young? Besides, I
wanted him to be free. I stood there, watching him
go down the long drive between the chestnut and the
lime trees. It was dusk, the sky touched with pink, and
a mist rising. Just before the bend in the drive, where
that one tree was struck with lightning, you know the
one I mean? – he turned and held up his hand in salu-
tation. I wanted to cry out but I didn't. I thought: this
is the last I shall see of him.

'I remember going out into the garden to do some
pruning. I couldn't bear to go back into the house and
when I did it was to wander restlessly from room to
room. Everything was so full of his touch: the desk

where he wrote, the flowers he had picked that morning, the rumpled cushions where he had sat on the sofa after lunch trying to do a Chinese puzzle, and his sherry glass on the mantelpiece. At least I was alone. I could not have borne it had anyone been there.'

Love is indeed a many splendoured thing!

## 8 SEPTEMBER

*The Times* yesterday reported that the number of Anglicans attending church has fallen to a record low of 14 per cent. Those attending a weekly service have shrunk to 72,000. The drop has been most noticeable among 45–54 year olds. Among the over 55's this has fallen to 26 per cent, while the proportion of Roman Catholics between 1983 and 2017 has fallen from 10 per cent to 8 per cent. The number of those who say they have no religion has increased to 52 per cent, with 70 per cent of 18–24 year-olds citing no affiliation with any particular faith.

I am increasingly convinced that it is the churches as institutions that is at the heart of the dilemma, as well as forms of worship that are no longer meaningful. I am confident, however, that people will rediscover a deeper form of spirituality and, where Christianity is concerned, one that is closer to the teachings of Jesus.

9 SEPTEMBER

The walls of my bedroom are lined with framed paintings, prints, and calligraphy. Lying in my bed, on the right wall, I see in the glass of each picture a reflection of my French windows and the garden beyond. To me it is an image of the life beyond this present.

10 SEPTEMBER

I am rereading Florida Scott-Maxwell's book *The Measure of My Days*, which is a reflection on old age. She describes a group of women on a railway platform 'And then the train came in and we went our separate journeys. Perhaps that's it: each of us is on a journey. And for each, the journey into old age is different. It may be dreadful or, if we will, it can be glorious.' Later on she says, 'Forty years ago, when I was training to be a Jungian analyst, I had certain experiences of the deep unconscious that were numinous, convincing proof of order and meaning in the universe. I knew then that I had a place in that order, and I felt contained. Behind everything, my conviction that there is a meaning, as well as mystery, remains unchanged.' I echo those words! At one point she quotes some lines from Edwin Muir, a poet I have always loved,

'I have learned another lesson

When life's half done we must give quality
to the other half, else you lose both, lose all. Select,
select, make an anthology
of what's been given you by bold casual time.
Revise, omit; keep what's significant.'

In the evening the lodger comes in, switches off all
lights but one, and plays for us both, he lying on the
sofa, I in my armchair, the recent broadcast from the
Albert Hall of András Schiff playing Bach's 'Well Tem-
pered Clavier'. How strange to think it was originally
played on so soft and delicate an instrument as the
clavichord that is behind me, but which my fingers are
too clumsy any more to play. When the recording is
over I google to see if Rosalyn Tureck ever recorded it,
and she did! So I have ordered it. I have never forgotten
hearing her at the Festival Hall playing Bach's 'Gold-
berg Variations' on the piano and, at the end of that
long journey, she just sat quietly at the piano, resting
in the silence, until she turned to face us and then the
cheers broke out.

11 SEPTEMBER

If one walks across a field with a water diviner they
will know exactly where to tap into the water underground and sink a bore. Similarly there are times in
our lives when our lives appear parched and dry yet

underground are untapped resources. We have only to reach down into our own depths and wait for the water to bubble up.

I am up early as Edward is coming to create some kind of shield for the newly planted wallflowers. The squirrels came and dug them all up, hoping they were bulbs. The lodger replanted them for me, and put down chicken wire. The next day the squirrels were found to have tugged away the wire and dug up the plants again! The squirrels live at the top of the ash tree at the bottom of my garden. When I plant tulip and narcissi bulbs each autumn I have to cover each pot with chicken wire, weighted down with stones. The lawn here was once a field of pale mauve crocuses in the spring but the squirrels set to work digging up the bulbs. What purpose do squirrels have other than being pests? Who first introduced them into this country? And then they drove out the native red squirrel, and have gone on multiplying ever since! Once in Wales I put out daily special poison, warfarin, at the foot of the bird table, which was supposed to kill them. They just returned each day to eat more and more.

12 SEPTEMBER

Harry Burton sends me this delightful quote from Rumi:

'I didn't come here of my own accord, and I can't leave that way. Whoever brought me here will have to take me home.'

In today's *The Times* I read how two-thirds of American teenagers prefer to communicate with their friends online rather than face-to-face. This surely is going to affect marriages and more formal relationships, if couples can't talk face-to-face?

13 SEPTEMBER

It is like the first day of autumn, the sun shining, the air cool and fresh, as Edward works at various tasks in the garden.

I have been reflecting on old age, and find myself arrested by something St. Paul wrote about ageing: 'While our outer man is wasting away, our inner man is renewed each day.'

The important thing, as Karlfried Durckheim wrote, is to let go now, 'let go of what was until now the centre of your life. Leave it behind and start listening to what is inside you, allow your existential being to manifest itself. Begin to make your way to maturity.' It means staying true to the child within one, realising it is never too late to develop one's creativity. I accept now that I no longer direct or work with actors, no longer teach, no longer have a role, but yet I am still learning, still discovering, still exploring, especially by listening inwardly. One has to learn how to let go of one's past and accept that one will be diminished – in order to grow. This is what Jung refers to as 'individuation', returning to a deeper dimension of one's self; what Durckheim referred to as the essential being, and St. Paul as 'the inner man', or of course inner woman.

I am deeply engrossed in a book that is truly revelatory, called *Resurrecting Jesus*, by a Zen-Buddhist teacher, Adyashanti. It is as though one had never read the Gospels before. When prayers end with the phrase 'through Jesus Christ our Lord' it always makes me think of Jesus as a window through we see that which lies beyond.

Interestingly Harry Burton writes to me, 'At the moment I have taken to addressing the receiver of my prayers as 'Great Mystery beyond the Blue'. It seems to help to create a sense of direct and connected address, since it's such a fact-based appeal: beyond the visible blue of our sky, there stretches an incredible, unfathomable, invisible mystery, and our being here seems somehow related to it being out there!'

14 SEPTEMBER

Religion, like many institutions, needs to renew itself. We read in the Gospels how Jesus, a devout Jew, tried to breathe new life into the religion in which he grew up. The essence of his teaching was that each of us has a destiny, though often it is not what we expected!

15 SEPTEMBER

I love these cool days of autumn, but then I love all the seasons. With the spring comes new energy, trees and plants in bud, birds busy nesting. With the full heat of summer comes the bloom of roses and gardens at their peak. With autumn, after a blaze of colour, we see the leaves fall, revealing the outline of trees – a moment that always reminds me of some old people who, stripped of all their leaves, as it were, reveal their inner self.

I am rereading much of George Herbert, in preparation for preaching at my final Eucharist on Nov 11th, which is also my 91st birthday. It is my final celebration as my PTO (Permission to Officiate) expires, and I know I haven't the energy to fill in all the forms to renew it and spend a day listening to bureaucratic talks, which I have done in the past. I understand why, legally, the Church has to put its clergy through these hoops every few years, but not for me anymore. But among Herbert's poems I love certain phrases from the poem on prayer...

'Church bells beyond the stars heard, the soul's blood, the land of spices, something understood.'

16 SEPTEMBER

There is much that can't be recounted in these pages. Individuals find their way to me, either to share their burdens, or seeking feedback. So many people are lost, or deeply lonely. And while I have had years of good analysis and still, occasionally, take a dream to a Jungian analyst, to help me unpack it, I am not a qualified counsellor. My role is simple to listen and share people's burdens, problems, or anxieties; to listen totally. Often that is all that is needed: for one person to be able to share whatever is troubling them with someone who truly listens. And so I am here for whoever needs me. I also receive long emails from people I have never met, and I respond. And there are, of course, those who read my twice-monthly blogs on meditation and then write to me. One thing I am clear-eyed about is that I am not a guru or a sage. I know very little.

Friends have played such key roles in my life and I recall something that Dame Laurentia McLachlan OSB wrote to her friend Sir Sydney Cockerell: 'What a mystery friendship is! And how strangely and delightfully different one's friends are one from the other – not only in themselves, but in the way one has to look at them. Some we have to carry, while others carry us. The perfect friend, to my mind, is one who believes in one once and for all, and never requires explanations and assurances.'

## 17 September

On the news is the story of the Legaria Children's Home in the West of Scotland, which housed 40 children when in 1972 the Rev. William Barrie and his wife, Mary, were appointed superintendents. They began a reign of beating and raping the young girls. The story is told by three of those girls, now mature women, who were raped hundreds of times and loaned out to other pedophiles, and neither the police nor any authority would listen to the girls' pleas at the time, 'Please, Mr Barrie is hurting us!' Dozens were abused. Reading such a story, I think of the many thousands of children, especially boys, throughout the world who have been abused by Catholic priests.

## 18 September

Today I go to Amplifon to have new hearing aids fitted. It is going to make a large hole in my account but, as the lodger reminds me, 'There are no pockets in a shroud! It is the truth.'

James Hollis in his book *Creating a Life*, writes 'We have not just one life, but many lives to live, many tasks, many vocations.'

This has certainly been true of my life!

19 SEPTEMBER

In the morning Tony Morris calls to talk about my various writing projects as well as the future of the Bleddfa Centre for the Creative Spirit. I decide that I should assemble some 50 of my blogs over the past few years to make a book entitled *The Sound of Silence*, as a sequel to my book, *Finding Silence*.

In the afternoon Susan Wooldridge comes to tea, bearing heather plants and ginger biscuits. We have known each other for nearly thirty years. We first met when I interviewed her for my biography of Richard Wilson, as she had been in his film about amputees of the First World War. She played a nurse, and in one improvisation Richard had her scrubbing floors for two hours in the house where they were filming up in Scotland! She talks of the difficulty of going backstage to congratulate an actor on his or her performance. 'If one is too moved, often there are no words. And, if one thinks it terrible, what does one say!' I tell her how once in New York, when I was teaching at the Julliard School of Music in New York, Martha Hill, the Head of the Dance Department, invited me to join her to see a one-man show by a former student. It was terrible and she said, 'I don't know what to say!' However, when the dancer appeared, she threw her arms around him in a great embrace, saying the one word 'Luis!' Brilliant.

Susan later sends me via email Alan Bennett's brilliant piece, *Going Round*.

20 SEPTEMBER

I am much moved by some lines also of Charles Causely from a poem about his parents:

They beckon to me from the other bank.

I hear them call, 'See where the stream path is!

Crossing is not as hard as you might think'.

And I recall Hywel, in the last week of his life, though he couldn't speak and could only move his right arm, on two occasions lifting that arm and pointing ahead with urgency, his eyes aglow. Who, or what, was he seeing?

21 SEPTEMBER

To the Royal Free for my massage and Keith Hunt points to various bruises on my right thigh and leg, due to warfarin and where I have inadvertently knocked the leg. He warns me to be careful as an infection could set in.

22 SEPTEMBER

I find it interesting that Jesus simply invited two or three to gather together in His name. Wendell Berry observed that almost all the significant and religious events recounted in the Bible did not occur in temples made with hands. The great visionary encounters, from Abraham to Jesus, did not take place in temples but in sheep pastures, in the desert, in the wilderness, on mountains, on the shores of a river or a lake, in the middle of the sea, in a prison. And I recall the words of the present Dalai Lama, 'we have no need for great temples or complicated philosophies. Our heart is our temple and our kindness is our philosophy.'

What is so often lacking from worship is any sense of the sacred. It has all become too sanitised, too genteel, repeated by rote. It is we, however, who by our attention and concentration, hallow a place and make it sacred. But, as Wendell Berry observes, a sacred place does not have to be a special place. I think often of a letter written to me in her late seventies by my friend Sheila Rose, recalling an experience of some thirty years previous, and which she has never forgotten.

'Many years ago', she wrote, 'when our children were still young, we went up Midsummer Hill on the Malverns to see the sun rise on Mid-Summer's Day. We started off from our cottage at three in the morning and climbed silently while it was still dark. The dawn chorus was just starting and the air throbbed with bird song. At the summit were small groups of people already gathered: some young students still asleep in their sleeping bags, others softly strumming guitars.

There were no discordant sounds, no traffic, just a soft humming of voices to muted chords, and a great feeling of friendship. We were all drawn together, waiting for that perfect moment when the first sliver of red sun appeared. One held one's breath, one prayed. Then the guitars stopped and the voices fell silent as the sun rose. It was like the end of the world, so silent, and yet also the beginning. For with the rising of that glorious sun and the streaking of the dark sky with red and gold, a great sigh of joy and wonder spread among all those who were there, as the full light of day transformed that hilltop. Faces were flushed with delight, there were some tears of joy and such a sharing of a deep spiritual companionship that has forever stayed with us all. For a brief while we were cleansed of all inhibitions, fears and barriers. It was a worship and a celebration. God was present and touched us all. Silently we were reborn. Later, a happy crowd of us surged into the little hut on the top of the hill for breakfast, served especially for this morning. The fragrance of hot coffee, sizzling bacon, drifted across the hills. Never did a meal taste so good!'

## 23 SEPTEMBER

This evening to the Wigmore Hall to hear the Heath Quartet – the most memorable work being Beethoven's 'String Quartet in A Minor op.132'. At the start of the third movement I felt Hywel sitting beside me as he did so often at Wigmore recitals, and then suddenly he and I were walking through cornfields to watch the sun rise as birds flew about us on their invisible trajectories. Slowly others began to emerge from the woods to join us, all the people in both our lives, forming a great circle of praise to the rising sun, and then slowly starting to revolve, with shouts and cries of joy. A little later the huge crowd of us made our way through the woods, in small groups, talking, and looking forward to a celebratory breakfast. There was such joy in the air, such a sense of celebration. It was indeed a very special experience!

## 24 SEPTEMBER

I work most of the day editing the text of this book remembering always that less is more! When I wrote my memoirs I did twelve drafts, and of *A Life Shared*, seven drafts.

## 25 SEPTEMBER

I had sent to Alan Bennett a copy of A Life Shared reminding him of one particular evening when he came to our flat in Belsize Park with Patrick Garland. Also present were Kenneth Williams and Linda Thorson. Around midnight, while Kenneth was telling one of his stories and we were laughing, there came a loud knocking from below, as our neighbour Erica Seelig beat her ceiling with a stick, obviously unable to sleep because of the raucous sound of our hilarity!

Alan writes so movingly about my book, congratulating Hywel and me on our 54-year relationship, adding that he and Rupert have been together for 26 years. He says he would love to come and have a cup of tea with me.

A recent test in the Imaging Department of the University College Hospital has revealed that the lymph nodes in my neck have grown since the last examination but the doctor says I can be given injections that will reduce them in size.

26 September

A lost day.

27 September

Libby Purves arrives at noon, a rucksack on her back containing her laptop, books, etc. We have a lively two hours of sharing. She talks a little of how she and her husband Paul dealt with the trauma of their talented son's suicide. She is a deeply rooted person, and with great humour. The time whizzes by until she departs to review a season of Pinter plays at the Pinter Theatre.

28 SEPTEMBER

Another letter arrives from Elizabeth Halls saying how moved she was when reading my book, *A Life Shared*, by the description of Hywel's last illness and my being with him, and not just beside him. She then goes on to say how when her father was dying, he had Parkinson's disease:

'In those last weeks there was a translucence about him, moments of tremendous clarity of connection, in the eyes when he looked at me and I returned his gaze, or in some of the simple things he was able to say. There was so much love and we met at a deeper level than the usual ways in which we would bustle about each other in the full flow of life. I felt as if the essence of him was fully present and that's where we met. Even after he had slipped into a coma I felt a strength of connection that was greater than I had ever known with him, even though it was wordless. The word 'accompanying' someone through death certainly felt completely right. Love holds us powerfully when we seem outwardly powerless.'

All this I, too, experienced with Hywel in those last weeks.

## 29 September

I think how in my fifties I would almost always spend Nov 11th, my birthday, walking for a whole day on the Radnor Hills, quietly reflecting. Those days are long gone and walking now is no longer a pleasure, simply a necessity to get from A to B. Apart from the neuropathy in my feet, walking feels as though I am wading through thick mud up to my hips. It must be some form of rheumatism in the hips and lower back – yet I have an excellent Alexander lesson every week as well as a massage. But I don't complain, and make myself walk about a mile each day.

It is another clear, cool autumnal day and the lodger has a lunch party of friends, all of whom I know. One of the guests produces a card that the driver of her bus from Highgate gave to every passenger as they got off. It read: 'I would just like to say a big thank you! To all my passengers whether you said good morning driver! Hello driver! Or thank you, driver (it means a lot.) I have been working this route nearly 15 years and met some wonderful people, and as an act of solidarity, I would just like to say its been a pleasure serving you all – from the London Scottish driver

– I hope you have a happy stress free day! LOVE AND RESPECT FROM THE DRIVER X.' Such a gesture in this day and age is very moving indeed.

30 SEPTEMBER

Charley Duff (I have just bought two copies of his moving memoir, *Charley's Woods* to give to friends) has just given me Richard Holloway's latest book, *Waiting for the Last Bus – Reflections on Life and Death*. Clearly throughout his life he has been a deeply caring priest in spite of his many doctrinal doubts. He reminds me of my great friend John Hencher, an Anglican priest.

In a book of his reflections, entitled *Glimpses of a Life*, published after his death by his devoted friend John Cupper, he describes how as a boy the school was taken to a cinema in Worcester to be shown unedited and unexpurgated newsreels of the liberation of the Nazi camps of Auschwitz and Belsen. It was, he says, a horrifying experience. One of the cries, repeated many times was 'Where is God?'

'Where indeed!' John writes, 'Did all of this mean God was powerless, or indifferent or too far away? Where was the God to whom his people were of more value than many sparrows, one of whom would not fall without him? Was it all a beautiful myth, made to comfort us? Was the truth, in fact, simple? There is no God... Were the great theological works, the great buildings, the structure of the church, the huge influence of the Christian faith on history, on culture, on the arts all simply beautiful examples of man's inventiveness?'

These were the questions that he faced as a 14-year-old boy, 'and which now, 61 years later, remain unanswered. My time at theological college, my ordination, years of thought and study did nothing to provide any satisfactory answers.' Yet he was an exceptional and inspirational priest. In the end, and at the end, he joined the Quakers, finding a relief in their lack of formal creeds or statements and complete openness and acceptance of an individual approach to belief, with their liberal and powerful simplicity.

An answer to some of his questions regarding Belsen and Auschwitz are answered in Viktor Frankl's book, *Man's Search for Meaning*, in which he tells the story of his struggle for survival in Auschwitz and other Nazi concentration camps. The existence of a Divinity cannot be proved scientifically nor even intellectually: it requires a different kind of knowing, what James Hillman calls 'contemplative knowledge', though I would prefer the word 'Intuition'. Another word for this is, of course, 'gnosis.' As a small boy once said to me with great passion, 'God is a feel, not a think!'

# OCTOBER 2018

## 1 October

Dorothy Duffy has given birth to her first child. She tells me of her plans to plant trees in the future. I tell her about Ruth Pavey's book *A Wood of One's Own* in which she describes how she created a wood on the Somerset Levels. I send Dorothy a cheque suggesting she plant two trees, a Jimmie tree, and one for the lodger. I suggest she might get other friends to do likewise so that one day, with her daughter, she will be able to walk among her friends.

## 2 October

The post brings a letter from my friend Edward Storey, the poet. He writes that his liver cancer has been found to be in such an advanced state that surgery is out of the question, while the high level of chemotherapy needed to control it would itself be fatal.

'So now,' he says, 'it is a waiting game of weeks rather than months. I am calmly resigned to the inevitable and happy to know I can spend the rest of my time in the lovely surroundings of my own home rather than the lonely ward of a hospital among strangers. Angela and I are determined to live that time as normally as possible…
yours, beyond more than we know, Edward.'

## 3 OCTOBER

Johanna, one of our meditation group, recently loaned me various CDs of works by Bach, including several sonatas for viola da gamba and harpsichord, and I kept playing the latter over and over, it gave me such a joy.

## 4 OCTOBER

A reflection: when two friends or two lovers choose to live together there will be occasional clashes, irritation at certain habits or tics, but the secret is to accept these and not seek to change each other's ways. And for lovers this is even more important. I recall how early in my relationship with Hywel Jones there was one occasion when he said with some passion, 'You're my lover, not my teacher!' I never forgot that lesson.

## 5 OCTOBER

Massage at the Royal Free then back to prepare and cook a venison casserole for Sunday night when Lucy Letherbridge joins our meditation group.

## 6 OCTOBER

It is icy cold today and the pavements are littered with shrivelled brown leaves, signalling the start of autumn. As a boy I loved trudging through deep layers of autumn leaves in the woods, and once, at school aged nine, I did a drawing of myself with coloured pencils doing exactly this!

This week's copy of *The Tablet* has just arrived with a very important article by Maggie Fergusson reporting on the increasing number of lonely people. In the UK 7.7 million people live alone and they are those born between the mid 1940s and mid 1960s, the baby boomer generation. More than a million older people feel lonely all or most of the time. But loneliness, she stresses, is not confined to the elderly. She ends her article by quoting Mother Teresa of Calcutta, 'I think the greatest suffering in the world is being lonely, feeling unloved, just having no one. I have come more and more to realise that it is being unwanted that is the worst disease than any human being can experience. Being unwanted.'

And in the same issue of *The Tablet* is a brochure from the YMCA inviting one, at £12 a month, to help house homeless young people. I have at once filled in the form.

Anne comes for my Alexander lesson and says the difficulty I have in walking could be due to my heart, and so she has given me a new exercise. Selina comes to tea.

She and I have one of our richest sharings and I have ordered for her a copy of my book *Experimental Theatre*, still in print after 50 years. In the 1970s when I was doing extensive lecture tours across America, the paperback of this book was on sale in every airport.


7 OCTOBER


Everyone arrives for the meditation group and Dan gives the talk, a very honest and moving account of how he has been meditating for many years and in the first few years had many rich experiences but in the past two years none, and it has been a discipline to keep going.

After the Silence I comment how the practice of meditation is in some ways like the experience of being in love, which in the first years of a relationship is very heady, and then at intervals becomes humdrum; as Madeleine L'Engle wrote, 'The growth of love is not a straight line but a series of hills and valleys. I suspect that in every good marriage there are times when love seems to be over. Sometimes these desert lines are simply the only way to the next oasis. Most growth comes through times of trial.'

Reflecting about this later I recall how for forty years Mother Teresa of Calcutta lost all sense of God, yet she persevered in the work she was called to do. And so, in the practice of meditation, we simply plod on, but as I remark in *Finding Silence*, much is going on underground, in the depths of one's sub-conscious

## 8 OCTOBER

Off to the dentist, took just five minutes, all my teeth in good order. Back to welcome Edward who has come to mow the lawn and do other tasks. In going through papers I come across a story that I find very moving. Apparently the BBC made a film about this man in 2005, his name Cyril Axelrod. He was born deaf, and as a young man he established deaf schools in Macao and South Africa. In middle life he became blind and this meant he had to stop his work. He felt cut off by his double disability but he responded by learning massage and through touch learned to communicate without seeing and hearing people. He became a

professional masseur, and then took Holy Orders. As
Father Cyril he was the only deaf-blind priest in the
world. He had fully accepted his disabilities and found
a way that brought him the satisfaction of being able to
help his fellow beings at several levels. It is a marvellous
example of how we are here not for ourselves but for
others.

In sorting out letters I have come across one dated Jan
2007 from Gill Stephens in Abergavenny, who writes,
'I decided to introduce a new ritual into our family
Christmas Eve this year, inspired by your book, *Passages
of the Soul: Ritual Today*. I put a little crib in our wood
with a candle alight near it and when it was dark we
went out with the grandchildren, following a luminous
star held aloft on a pole, and singing 'We three Kings
of Orient are'. I led them round the walnut tree and up
into the wood and then we stood by the crib and sang
'Away in a manger'. We then carried the crib back to the
house and put it near the Christmas tree. The children,
and their parents, uncles and aunts, were thrilled by it.
My son wanted it to stay outside with the candle burning as a place to go to alone, and know it was there as a
light burning in the darkness outside.'

9 OCTOBER

The early dark nights have begun which always make
me want to retire early. Last night the small park at the

end of the garden was floodlit all night – this has happened before and I wonder why? Is it to deter potential burglars to all the houses such as this which surround the park, and which is not open to the general public, but available only for use by children from local schools during the day-time?

The lodger spends time each day in the conservatory doing his tax returns. Mine were done a month ago and simply await Nick Beardwood to collect.

## 10 October

All summer London, and doubtless the rest of the country, has been plagued by fruit flies. They stand out on the shining white tiles of my bathroom like specs of soot and I regularly squash them. I asked the lodger how they breed and he replied, 'in the usual way!' but it is difficult to think of one tiny fly on top of another, but the same must be so for blue-bottles, wasps, spiders. I then begin to think about tortoises and hedgehogs copulating and the whole thing becomes very curious. Doubtless somewhere someone has written a paper on the subject.

## 11 October

Another glorious autumn day and the virginia creeper at the bottom of the garden, that falls like a curtain

over my study there, is like a tapestry of rich colours
– which reminds me that this weekend the lodger is
doing a two-day weaving course.

A friend of many years comes to lunch. His wife
died about five years ago of cancer. She was in intensive
care for six months and he visited daily. He was shat-
tered by her death, but of late, he tells me, she has been
appearing in his dreams and always he wakes feeling
very happy. This may be the work of the unconscious,
as I also experienced after the death of Hywel, or it may
signal that those who have died are telling us that there
is a life beyond. We shall each of us discover one day
whether this is so or not!

12 OCTOBER

Last night I vomited and had the runs so the lodger
suggested I have a long soak in the bath – usually I am
in and out within four minutes. I retired to bed with
a hot-water bottle. The lodger is very wise about such
matters and I have learned to heed his advice.

This morning I was woken by a gentle tap on the
door – it was 10 30 – and there was the lodger, just off
to work, with a tray on which was a ramekin filled with
chopped walnuts soaked in honey, and a cup of tea.

I have stayed in bed all day, not having much energy.
But all shall be well and all manner of things shall be
well.

## 13 October

All day in bed, but the lodger has brought in supplies of food in case I feel peckish.

This evening when he returned from a day of learning to weave he insisted on making me a light collation with a glass of wine, recommended a long soak in the bath, and a change of pyjamas; then, once I was in bed, he brought me a hot-water bottle wrapped in a towel.

I have also been reflecting how it is possessiveness that often destroys a relationship. It's important to realise that we can never own another human being. Some come into our lives like migrant birds, and then, in due course, fly off on the rest of their journey. We have to learn to let them go. The exception of course is where a couple have children. Then whatever the difficulties, these have to be worked through, perhaps with the help of a marriage counsellor. As I have remarked before, so much psychological damage is done to small children when one parent walks away. Some never recover from the effects and in later life repeat the same mistakes. All relationships call for work, discipline, and deep caring of each for the other and for the relationship itself.

## 14 October

In bed most of the day, little energy. Went to heat up the pork casserole for my supper but it was too rich and I threw it away and instead had smoked salmon.

## 15 October

Today I get up, dress, go to the shops and work on my homily for the Last Eucharist I shall celebrate on 11 November.

I find myself shocked by the recent wedding of Princess Eugenie and husband. I am neither a monarchist nor a republican, but the fact that the policing required is estimated to cost the taxpayer between two to four million pounds, at such a time of political uncertainty, strikes me as totally insensitive. She is but ninth in line to the throne, for heaven's sake! How much more fitting and sensitive had they both said we want to be married quietly, but if photographers want to photograph us coming out of church that is fine.

## 16 October

I have been reflecting on relationships, whether in an office or work situation, or in a close relationship: parent and child, teacher and pupil, friend and friend or lovers. How quickly friction can arise: some minor irritation lights a tinder. It may be one's tone of voice is misinterpreted and what is said is taken as an accusation. Sometimes, when an individual is tired or under stress, they may speak sharply, and when that happens the other must not respond in kind. In any relationship there will be these small pinpricks. As Odd, the small bear, in one of my Odd and Elsewhere books, says to his friend Elsewhere, the clown, 'There are up days and down days and today is one of my down days!' The secret is not to overreact. It is fatal to respond in kind!

Sometimes, when two people decide to live together, at first they have so much in common but slowly differences will appear. It might be that one is domestically tidy and the other the total opposite, or one is a late night owl and the other an early bedder. In this household the lodger is an owl and I am more like a clucking hen, early to roost. The important thing to remember is that one can never change another person. Change can only come from within. One other reflection: if one person makes a wounding remark, never to retaliate with another wounding remark for, in no time at all, there will be an emotional conflagration in which terrible things are said, and as one reads regularly in the press, even murder, as emotions get out of hand. It is here that the practice of some form of meditation is invaluable, preventing one from being overwhelmed by emotion.

There comes into my mind those lines of Burns, 'to

see ourselves as others see us'. When I was young and insecure I was often bumptious, and pushy. I remember John Cullen, who worked for Methuen, telling me I must stop name-dropping. It is true I had met, albeit briefly, the names I mentioned, usually through being taken backstage by Eleanor Farjeon to meet the star of the show. I realised I was name-dropping in order to boost my ego. I have been fortunate therefore in having a number of friends who have not shirked holding the mirror up to my behaviour.

17 OCTOBER

I have been reading *Christian Beginnings, from Nazareth to Nicea AD 30–325* by Geza Vermes, published in 2012. He concludes with the following fascinating observation: after reading this book 'those readers who wonder where they now stand should remember that in the sixteenth century the rediscovery by Renaissance scholars of the ancient sources of classical civilisation forced Christians to return to the Bible for a revitalisation and purification of their faith. This revolution first created Protestantism, but subsequently spread over the whole spectrum of the churches. It would seem that by now it has reached, or will soon reach, a stage when a fresh revival will be called for, a new 'reformation', zealous to reach back to the pure religious vision and enthusiasm of Jesus, the Jewish charismatic messenger of God, and not to the deifying message Paul, John and the church attributed to him.' I find such an observation wonderfully refreshing and deeply perceptive.

Thanks to the ministrations of the lodger I am recovered from two bouts of illness, which left me very weak, but now the energy surges back like a river in full spate!

18 OCTOBER

Another lost day!

19 OCTOBER

Just off to have my weekly massage and then shopping for the weekend plus photocopying Lucy Lethbridge's excellent review of both my books in the November issue of The Oldie.

Out walking I am much more conscious these days of being an old man. I am not depressed, but think of Yeats' lines:

An aged man is but a paltry thing,
A tattered coat upon a stick, unless
Soul clap its hands and sing, and louder sing
For every tatter in its mortal dess,
Nor is there singing school but studying
Monuments of its own magnificence;

And therefore I have sailed the seas and come
To the holy city of Byzantium.

– And the poem has also that wonderful phrase,

'and gather me
Into the artifice of eternity.'

## 20 OCTOBER

So many today die from the effect of hurricanes, tor-
nadoes, tsunamis and flooding; so many vast numbers
are immigrants, emigrants, beggars or homeless; so
many succumb to dementia or Alzeimer's, many are
crippled in horrendous accidents, or are born deformed,
and while the planet is in danger of overbreeding parents are still bringing children into this troubled world,
increasingly having double births. Where is it all leading and, as many will say, where is God in all this? It
is not surprising that in this country, and in Ireland,
more and more people are becoming agnostic, and
the Christian references on which I and others were
brought up are increasingly discarded. It is a gloomy
picture, and a deeply disturbing one, begetting in
so many an attitude of cynicism, and a 'me' culture,
everyone out for themselves. And yet, in spite of all this,
I find I have an underlying faith that there is a pattern
and a purpose.

Anne comes to give me my Alexander lesson and then helps me take cuttings from the geraniums and pot them all, against the winter. I work on my homily for my final Eucharist on Nov. 11th – 'the breaking of the staff' as our splendid Vicar, Marjorie Brown remarked. I also intend to make cuts in the liturgy – it is far too wordy and there is need for more space and silence. As it is the last time I shall celebrate the Eucharist I am unlikely to be summoned before the Bishop or even burned at the stake! The great thing about St. Mary's, Primrose Hill, is that it is open to change, and often, under its previous Vicar, John Ovenden, I was encouraged to experiment.

Too much of the language used in the liturgy has remained rooted in the past, and many of the rituals are mere husks of what was once a living reality.

21 OCTOBER

Another gentle autumn day. I spend much time in the kitchen preparing the roast pork for Norman tonight.

22 OCTOBER

To The Garrick Club for a piano recital of Schubert and Liszt by the Dutch pianist, Camiel Boomsma. Always I have seats reserved in the front row of the Morning Room, and it is a great privilege to hear and observe music being played at such close quarters, as it would have been in private homes in the 18th century and into the early 19th century.

## 23 OCTOBER

There is a line from a poem by Robert Frost,

'What to make of a diminished thing?'

That's the thought that comes to me and I imagine to most elderly people. My sense of taste, smell, and hearing are affected by old age, and though I have good hearing aids which work well with one or two people, if there is a crowd, I can't hear what is being said to me. I am also aware of the physical changes in my body, and also how dull I can be in conversation. Obviously the latter was not always so, since I have had, and still have, a rich range of friends, but the need to talk is now far less. I love the companionship of the lodger and our shared conversations from time to time but, in the main, I prefer to listen to people. There was a time when I toured America for several years, speaking to Women's Clubs and lecturing at Colleges, just as I have delivered many sermons, but each of these was written and learned by heart in the way that an actor learns and performs a role. But I lack the gift of spontaneous chat such as the lodger and a number of my friends have.

There is also no longer the need to talk so much but simply to rest in silence. This process of diminishment is perfectly natural, a gradual letting go. At such a time in one's life, says Teilhard de Chardin, God is in some way hollowing us out. Shedding, shedding, is not sad, but brings a deep contentment. I am so deeply grateful for friends – even those who speak sharply to me!

## 24 OCTOBER

John Atterbury and Ken Bryers come to lunch and we exchange stories about Hywel, whom they both knew, as well as many theatre anecdotes, and I find I suddenly sparkle, telling various tales that make them laugh! So perhaps I am not quite as dull as I often think I am. They both worked with Hywel at the Royal Opera House and describe how he would have them in fits of laughter in the dressing room with his stories.

I write to Edward Storey who, in spite of the specialists saying his cancer was too far advanced for them to operate and that he should go home to die, writes to me in his strong firm hand to say he has had three operations under local anaesthetic, during which in order to remain calm he mentally recited many poems!

## 25 October

Sharon comes to clean, and Edward to garden, while I do a fifth editing of this book up to the present moment.

I have been thinking about the occasions when I drop something and shout 'Fuck!' It has, I now see, no reflection on one's practice of meditation, but through the sound one releases the frustration and is once again calm. Those who look after the very elderly should not be fazed by such explosions, for they are healthy expressions of frustration. They shouldn't be bottled up!

## 26 October

Johanna Roeber, who recently gave me a CD of some of Bach's sonatas for viola da gamba and harpsichord has now organised for Sunday January 25th a recital of these sonatas at the Royal Academy of Music, played by two of their outstanding pupils. I am also to do 15 minutes speaking love poems. I say speak rather than read, as there is a huge difference between the two. The secret is to learn a poem by heart and then speak it fifty or more times, sometimes on a whisper, testing it in different ways, so that on the night one can speak it from the very centre of one's being. This, I recall Esmé Percy telling me, is how Sarah Bernhardt, under whom he studied, would prepare her part in a play: every nuance, emphasis, would be gone over again and again 'and only then would she go on stage and allow the Holy Spirit to take over!' One should never be aware of the actor acting!

This morning I had my weekly massage with Keith Hunt, head of the physiotherapy unit at the Royal Free. He told me how this morning he queued from 8 to 10 30 to get a £25 ticket to the new production of Stephen Sondheim's Company, rather than a £95 ticket! On my return Tusse appears to trim my toenails!

## 27 OCTOBER

The window cleaner arrives with his assistant to do the conservatory, my bedroom, and the lodger's room. Tony comes to mend the light in the passageway, then the lodger and Anne arrive at almost the same time, each telling me I must not go out as it is bitingly cold. It is almost too cold to concentrate, but I put some bubble wrap around the base of the large and still flowering geranium in the pot next to the statue of St. Benedict. In the morning I must wrap horticultural fleece around the two large urns. As I type this the lodger is seated in the conservatory, detailing his accounts for his accountant. Tomorrow I shall make a lamb casserole – I prepared everything today but didn't cook it, as the lodger, having been to Borough Market, had returned with delicious pork paté, freshly made, with crusty bread and sweet cornichons followed by a rich creamy cheese!

My friend T writes about the problems with her new partner, with whom she does not live, but who is inclined to be very demanding, and she realises she needs space and time to herself. I am reminded of what Kahlil Gibran writes in his book *The Prophet*, 'Let there be spaces in your togetherness.'

As the press has recently reported – loneliness appears to be a common experience for more and more in our community. The formation of groups such as a book group, a painting, quilting or a meditation group, etc. can help to foster a sense of community, of being part of a family. But in the end we have to accept that loneliness is part of the human condition, and the challenge for each one of us is how to respond to it, how to learn from it. As Emily Dickinson wrote:

'Loneliness is the maker of souls.'

This is why some form of daily meditation is important, as we learn to deal with silence and solitude. There is a story from the Desert Fathers of one young monk asking an older how he learned to be so still. He replied, 'From my cat, the way he sits by the mouse hole waiting!'

This reminds me of a poem dated c. 800 in *The Finest Music*, an anthology of early Irish lyrics. The poem is entitled 'Myself and Pangur', and is translated by Helen Waddell.

I and Pangur Bàn my cat,
Tis a like task we are at.
Hunting mice is his delight,
Hunting words I sit all night.

## 28 OCTOBER

Today at the Bleddfa Centre in Powys Marina Cantacuzino is giving the annual Bleddfa Lecture. We first
met when she left school and came to be my assistant at
Greenwich Theatre on two plays by Noel Coward that
I was directing. Then a few years later, she said, 'Will
you marry me?' and for a brief moment I thought, 'Is
this Leap Year?' And then realised she was asking me,
only recently ordained, to marry her to Dan Levy. For
many years she was a top journalist, until she founded
what has become a worldwide movement, *The Forgiveness Project*, the prime aim of which is to share stories
of forgiveness in order to build hope, empathy and
understanding. Past speakers for the Bleddfa annual
lecture, include the Rt. Rev Dr Rowan Williams, Sir
Peter Maxwell Davies, Libby Purves, Neil MacGregor,
Satish Kumar, and others.

## 29 OCTOBER

Reading some of the latest theological studies I find
authors still referring to God as 'he'. This has dogged

Christianity for centuries and resulted in a dominant male structure in the Catholic Church. Even the word 'Abba' has been mistranslated as 'Father' – Our Father. But Abba is an Aramaic word (that being the language Jesus spoke), which carries several meanings, rather as Chinese ideograms do. It means Parents, Mother and Father, and it also carries the meaning of source and origin of all things. So when I pray the Lord's Prayer I say 'Abba, Mother, Father, Source and Origin of all things, hallowed be Thy name.' It is interesting that the Gnostics understood this. They viewed the One which they called the true and unknown God as having a feminine part and this duality was centred in their creation myths, incorporating echoes of Taoism and the principles of Yin-Yang.

30 OCTOBER

I have been reflecting how effervescent is the art of theatre. Painters, sculptors, writers, photographers, composers are all able to leave their work behind them, but once a theatre production or a particular performance comes to an end it disappears into a vague memory. When the Martha Graham Company first came to London I went to every performance and met Martha Graham herself. It made a huge impact on me as a nascent director. Similarly I recall Tanaquil Le Clerc and Francisco Moncion dancing Balanchine's version of *L'Apres Midi* in New York, and the solo modern dancer Sybil Shearer, just as I recall certain performances in the drama.

But it is well nigh impossible to capture in words for future generations such experiences.

Why is theatre so elusive? Even when a production is filmed it is not the same. Theatre depends upon the physical presence of an audience and actors; what is happening is a shared experience. Theatre is made by people and executed by people. The filming of a theatre performance can never be the same as when experienced in the presence of others. As Peter Brook observes in *There are No Secrets*, 'The essence of theatre is within a mystery called 'the present moment.''

He also makes the important observation that a theatre experience which lives in the present moment 'must be close to the pulse of the time' which is why I have no doubt that the modern dance works of Martha Graham, which were so revolutionary at the time, might well seem dated today.

There is a line running through my head, which is from a poem entitled 'The Schoolmaster' by Yevtushenko. It speaks for me at this moment: 'I am old Auntie dear, you can't do much about growing old!' One has patiently to accept the gradual diminishings that are a part of ageing. It is all part of the stripping down to the absolute essentials, to the very essence of one's being.

31 OCTOBER

Yesterday the lodger spent an hour dealing with Scottish Power for me, whose charges have risen dramatically. The man at the other end had such a soft Scottish accent I could barely hear him.

In the night, lying in my bed I become, as so often, aware of Hywel's presence, and I murmur into the darkness the words 'Blessed be Hywel, blessed be the name of Hywel'. It is as Eliot says in *Little Gidding*, 'the communication of the dead is tongued with fire beyond the language of the living.'

# NOVEMBER 2018

## 1 November

John Donne wrote 'No man is an island, entire of itself'.

We are all inseparably linked, no one lives alone. In varying ways we are all interdependent on one another.

It is still very cold and also raining, but this evening to the Wigmore Hall with the lodger to hear a recital by a young pianist Federico Colli who is a brilliant exponent of Mozart and Scarlatti.

Absolutely dazzling, spellbinding in his brilliance, his quality of listening, and not being afraid to hold silence between sections of a work. This was his first performance at the Wigmore, and he received encore after encore!

## 2 November

The lodger asks me what I would like for my birthday but I don't need anything! He then says would I like to go on a cruise to Norway or America, or visit Greenland, but I have no desire to travel any more which I can see puzzles him. I used to be more adventurous but I think that age and my medication inhibits me. I recall inviting my mother to one of my first nights in the West End and she said no for the same reason and also for having to meet so many new people. I am happy to be where I am. After all, I have a whole interior world to explore!

Marina Cantacuzino writes to say the church was packed for the Bleddfa Annual Lecture and as part of her talk about *The Forgiveness Project* she invited Marian Partington to tell her story which made the occasion very special and moved people deeply. Marian's sister Lucy's remains were found 21 years after her disappearance buried under the floor of the house of Frederick West. She has written about this in her book, *If You Sit Very Still*, and described how she found healing from Quaker and Buddhist practices.

After the talk a woman came up to Marina to tell her how she had experienced a very similar trauma: her daughter, also ironically called Lucy, had been brutally murdered at the age of 25 just over twelve years ago. They bonded over the loss and have arranged to meet again, so as Marina says, some real healing took place in Bleddfa last Sunday which was amazing to witness. She also sends a photograph of she and Danny seated on Hywel's bench in the orchard. It is the bench I unveiled in Hywel's memory and his ashes are scattered in the orchard, as mine will be one day too.

## 3 NOVEMBER

John Rowlands-Pritchard has just sent me a superb piece of calligraphy on white canvas stretched on a wooden frame. I have so much of his work here but this is among some of his best. The words I came across a long time ago. They are:

'I have always known that I would take this road but I did not know it would be today.'

In my final homily at the final Eucharist, I shall be celebrating at St. Mary's, Primrose Hill, on November 11th, my 91st birthday. I want to look at the trajectory of Jesus' life, and why it took him thirty years before he discovered what he was meant to do with his life. Today with people living much longer, such a crisis often arises around the age of 40, when suddenly an individual perceives what his, or her, real life work is meant to be. It is both an exhilarating and testing discovery. The aim of each one us is to be able to say, whether we are believers or not, as Jesus did after less than three years of his teaching, 'Abba, I have done the work you gave me to do.'

Thinking back over my life I recall the pain of my early twenties, when I was up at Oxford, not knowing whether I was meant to be a monk, an actor, a writer or teacher; at that stage I knew nothing about being a theatre director. It has taken a series of errors and false turnings to realise and accept that I am all these roles, and the challenge has been how to weave these seemingly disparate strands into one pattern. It is very like the task faced by a director on the first day of rehearsal: how to weld a group of highly individual actors into an ensemble so that each complements the other.

## 4 November

Reflecting on what I wrote yesterday I can imagine some saying but how does one go about integrating the different, and sometimes opposing, parts of one's self? The answer will be different for each individual. For myself it was the years of rich Jungian analysis, plus more than fifty years practising meditation. And the work of integration, or what Jung termed individuation, continues right up to the end!

Today is our meditation day, and Pat Kaufman gives a very powerful talk about the themes of light and darkness in meditation.

Reflecting further on the words, 'I have always known that I would take this road but yesterday I did not know it would be today,'

What so often seems like the end of a story is, in fact, the beginning of a new one! We need to be ready to travel lightly and be open to change. A new pattern is so often at such times beginning to emerge.

5 NOVEMBER

This evening, being Guy Fawkes night, is a little like being on the Front Line, constant explosions of another kind of fireworks. I make a large quantity of mush-room paté (onions, mushrooms and rosemary) for a dinner party the lodger is planning next week.

7 NOVEMBER

I never cease to give thanks to Masha Rollings, the Jungian analyst I attended weekly in New York in 1955 to 1956, who first suggested I keep a journal. 'You are a lonely person,' she said, 'and keeping a journal is like talking to a most intimate friend.'

8 NOVEMBER

I find myself reflecting how when one loves, or is in love, one is the more easily wounded, and yet, because one loves, one works one's way through these rough passages. In general with our friends we are on our best behaviour, going out for a meal or a drink, or for a walk, and for those few hours we sparkle, but when two individuals choose to cohabit, the situation changes. You become aware of different emotional weathers, how one partner may speak sharply because he, or she, is worried about finances, or lack of work, or simply under the weather and that is when we begin to see each other in our entirety. The ragged ends, the sharp retorts, the grumbles, as well as the affection and concern. Hywel was a typical Cancerian and at intervals would totally withdraw into a mood that might last days. At first I felt he was perhaps bored with me, but gradually I began to understand that this was part of his psychological make-up and was in no way personal.

The sun shines, so I plant the tulip bulbs in the urns either side of the statue of St. Benedict and then cover with chicken wire to prevent the squirrels digging them up.

9 NOVEMBER

I put on my trainers to go shopping, but the right foot is so uncomfortable that I remove the shoe, thinking there may be grit. There is nothing so I put on the shoe again and with my trolley go to shop. Suddenly, looking down I observe I have put the left shoe on the right foot, and vice versa! So I sit on someone's steps, remove my shoes and place each on the right foot. Another example of one of the hazards of old age!

Considering this is the last day but one in this record of a year it is perhaps disappointing that I have nothing special to report! Cards and gifts begin to flow in for my 91st birthday, including a splendidly practical gift of thermal socks and a neck holder from my friend Joanna in Gloucestershire, and from Celia – a book by her brother, the Sufi master, Llewellyn Vaughan-Lee with Hilary Hart, entitled *Spiritual Ecology – 10 Practices to Reawaken the Sacred in Everyday Life*. I have most of his books on my shelves. The essence of Sufism is that we come from God and we go to God. However we may define that three letter word, there is this sense that there is a power, an energy, an intelligence, behind the universe.

The lodger brings me a large bottle of whisky for my cold, telling me that a glass each night is the best of all remedies. It is as good as living with one's own private doctor!

10 NOVEMBER

And tomorrow I mark my 91st year by celebrating my final Eucharist and preaching my last homily at the 8 o'clock service at St. Mary's.

What lies ahead is quite unknown, how many more years I have awaiting me, but the end certainly approaches! As I said at the start of this journal, I have no fear of dying, and am ready to depart when the time comes. I have not wasted my life but lived it to the full.

In my original production of Hugh Whitemore's *The Best of Friends* with John Gielgud and Rosemary Harris, the part of Bernard Shaw was played by a wonderful Irish actor, Ray McAnally. When some years later I directed a revival with Patricia Routledge and Michael Pennington, the part of Shaw was played by Roy Dotrice, then in his eighties, returning to the English stage after decades in Hollywood. He had already played the part in New York and won splendid reviews. In rehearsal of the second act I found him playing it slower and slower while his last line, 'I am going to die now' was spoken in a very downbeat manner. I said, no, no, no! It was becoming like a funeral. In real life Shaw's energy, his appetite for life and intellectual curiosity stayed with him to the end. Indeed, in the week before he died he was in his garden stoking a great bonfire and laughing! To his credit, and being such a fine actor, Roy at once applied my note and spoke the last line with an energy of excitement, eager to learn what lies beyond this existence. And so it also is for me!

One morning recently I woke with a deep sense of my ship coming in to harbour at long last. It reminded me of a painting by Margaret Neve entitled 'Homecoming'. It depicts a night sky with a huge full moon reflected on the ocean and in the centre of this halo of light is an old-fashioned galleon coming in to harbour. Is it Ulysses finally returning after his long journey? On the quayside, their backs to us, are five figures in long robes awaiting his return. And it will be likewise for each of us when we die?

I think of Cafavy's poem 'Ithaca', translated here by Rae Dalvern, about one's long voyage to Ithaca for which we have been aiming but, when we arrive, it has nothing more to give us:

'Ithaca has given you the beautiful voyage,

Without her you would never have taken the road,

But she has nothing more to give you.

And if you find her poor, Ithaca has not defrauded you.

With the great wisdom you have gained, with so much experience,

You must surely have understood by then what Ithaca means.'

None of this implies that I am about to die but the readiness is all. I have had such a full life, blessed with so much love. No wonder St. Teresa of Avila wrote, 'The important thing is not to think too much, but to love too much.'

*FINIS*

Along the way to knowledge,
Many things are accumulated.
Along the way to wisdom
Many things are discarded.
Less and less effort is used,
Until things arrange themselves.

*Lao-Tzu*

## ACKNOWLEDGEMENTS

I want to thank especially Tony Morris who first had the idea and the title for this book; Norman Coates for an early editing of the script, Tusse Silberg for patiently typing, and those friends who have given permission to quote from their letters and emails – and also the lodger, with gratitude for their continued support and friendship. I would also like to thank my editor, George Tomsett.

## ABOUT THE AUTHOR

JAMES ROOSE-EVANS' list of accomplishments is formidable. Fifty years ago he founded the Hampstead Theatre. He has written twenty-one books, including the best-selling *Inner Journey: Outer Journey* and *Experimental Theatre*, and has directed countless plays, including his award-winning adaptation of 84 Charing Cross Road. He is a non-stipendiary Anglican priest, founded the Bleddfa Centre for the Creative Spirit (in North Wales) and continues to lead meditation, ritual and theatre masterclasses today. He lives in Hampstead, north London.

## ALSO BY JAMES ROOSE-EVANS

Directing a play, foreword by Vanessa Redgrave

Experimental Theatre, (still in print after more than 40 years)

London Theatre: from the Globe to the National

One Foot on the Stage, the biography of Richard Wilson

Inner Journey: Outer Journey, with foreword by Rowan Williams. New editon 2019

Passages of the Soul: Ritual Today

The Cook-a-Story-Book, foreword by Gordon Ramsey

Opening Doors and Windows, a memoir

Finding Silence, foreword by Mark Tully

Blue Remembered Hills – A Radnorshire Journey

A Life Shared

Darling Ma, the letters of Joyce Grenfell to her mother, edited

The Time of my Life, the wartime journals of Joyce Grenfell, edited

CHILDREN'S BOOKS:

The Adventures of Odd and Elsewhere
The Secret of the Seven Bright Shiners
Odd and the Great Bear
Elsewhere and the Gathering of the Clowns
The Return of the Great Bear
The Secret of Tippity-Witchit
The Lost Treasures of Wales

STAGE ADAPTATIONS:

84 Charing Cross Road, by Helene Hanff
Cider with Rosie, by Laurie Lee
The Story of My Life, by August Hare

RADIO:

The Female Messiah, entered by the BBC for the Italia
    Prize
Topsy and Turvy (Gordon Craig and Isadora Duncan)
The Third Adam, by Jerzy Peterkiewicz

STAGE ENTERTAINMENTS THAT HAVE TOURED:

The Pride of Players – about the actors of the 19th
    century
A Celebration of Gardens

Kilvery with Flowers – the journals of Rev. Francis
   Kilvert
The Journey Thus Far

IN PREPARATION:

Loving – reflections on love
Anecdote – Age, a sequel to 'Older'

James writes a fortnightly blog
of thoughts and inspirations:

www.jamesrooseevans.co.uk